Palaces of Memory

American Composer Diane Thome on her Life and Music

Diane Thome

◆ FriesenPress

Suite 300 – 990 Fort St
Victoria, BC, V8V 3K2
Canada

www.friesenpress.com

Copyright © 2016 by Diane Thome
First Edition — 2016

All rights reserved.

Article by music critic Melinda Bargreen – Seattle Times, November 24, 2002
Permission given by Melinda Bargreen, October, 2015

Rumi poem, Who says Words with My Mouth, THE ESSENTIAL RUMI, p.2
Translation by Coleman Barks
Permission given by Coleman Barks, December 2015

Poem by Emily Dickinson, The grass so little has to do
from POEMS BY EMILY DICKINSON
Boston: Roberts Brothers, 1890
PS1541 A6 1890, Special Collections, University of Washington Libraries

Excerpt from WOMEN COMPOSERS and MUSIC TECHNOLOGY in the UNITED STATES by
Elizabeth Hinkle-Turner, 2006
Permission given by Elizabeth Hinkle-Turner, March 2016

Excerpts from works by Sri Aurobindo
Permission given by Sri Aurobindo Ashram Trust, December 2015

Chapter icons sourced from the Noun Project:
Common Time by Dilon Choudhury, Treble Clef by Catherine Please,
Bass Clef by Rhys de Dezsery, and Eighth Note by Rhys de Dezsery.

ISBN
978-1-4602-8429-2 (Hardcover)
978-1-4602-8430-8 (Paperback)
978-1-4602-8431-5 (eBook)

1. Music, Individual Composer & Musician

Distributed to the trade by The Ingram Book Company

TABLE OF CONTENTS

Palaces of Memory is the story of a pioneer in the music world – the first woman to graduate from Princeton University with a PhD in Music and the first woman to compose computer-synthesized music. Much has been written about Dr. Thome, now professor emerita and former chair of the composition program at the University of Washington School of Music. But this is Diane Thome's highly personal story about her lifelong journey in music.

In this inspiring memoir, Dr. Thome describes her studies with many famous teachers including Dorothy Taubman, Robert Strassburg, Milton Babbitt, Roy Harris and Darius Milhaud. She writes of a consuming need to compose and explore new directions in her music. She also writes with deep affection and candor about her many friends and great loves.

Diane Thome's music has been described as "high modernist ... searching, intense, and full of integrity." Much the same can be said of her life as it unfolds in *Palaces of Memory*.

Preface

At a certain time in one's life, it seems fitting and appropriate to take a larger and longer view of the significant changes and events that have characterized that life. This process also encourages a certain objectivity and detachment not always possible at a younger age. Perhaps an additional goal is to integrate one's experience, metaphorically painting it on a larger canvas. All these elements are the motivations that led me to undertake the writing of a memoir at this time in my life.

I wrote this memoir for a number of reasons. Most importantly, my life as a composer has spanned a significant period of twentieth century musical history. My electroacoustic music is emblematic of a major technological revolution for composers. My academic life can shed light on the role and significance of the American university in the lives of composers. Finally, the artistic and intellectual worlds I inhabited may serve as an inspiration for younger generations.

Naturally, there is the important and critical component of my personal story. Writing this memoir has only increased my gratitude to family, teachers, and special friends for their invaluable contributions to the privileged and remarkable life I have led. In addition, the factor of timing was immensely fortuitous, particularly in the unfolding opportunities of my professional career. Concurrently, while the influence of gender inequality and sexism was hardly absent from my life, new trails were being blazed. I would like to think that I made some small contribution to this paradigm change for women artists. This topic is explored in some depth in Chapter Four.

I cannot complete this introduction without mentioning the pleasure and satisfaction I received from thirty-two years of teaching and interacting with a variety of students at different levels and from diverse backgrounds. As I write in this memoir, I was exceedingly fortunate to be on the faculty of a large school of music in a major research university at a time when contemporary music and the performance of contemporary repertoire at an outstanding level were so highly valued. The sense of community I experienced with colleagues and students can never be taken for granted.

Finally, I wish to acknowledge the many gifts of my family, friends, life partners, colleagues, and students who nourished a magical and fulfilling life.

Diane Thome
January 2016

Chapter One

AN ARTISTIC DESTINY:

HOW MY MUSICAL LIFE BEGAN

Music has determined the architecture of my life and for this I am immensely grateful. My first debt of gratitude naturally goes to my parents who, despite the vicissitudes of their own lives, gave their four children opportunities to discover their individual interests and freedom to pursue them. The different environments in which I grew up – I had moved four times by the age of eleven – were full of books, records, radio opera broadcasts, and occasional concerts or visits to the ballet, all fostering my love of music. But how did it begin, this passionate life endeavor? I do not have complete answers.

My mother, trained as a child psychologist, told me that I was entranced with music from an unusually early age. When I was six and a half months old, she heard me experimenting with sounds in my crib. She relates that she observed my singing discrete tones, gradually moving higher and higher, until I got up as far as I could go. Then, she says, "You let out a little exclamation of delight." Obviously, I have no memory of this joyous infant discovery, but as a young child I was acutely sensitive to voices. A harsh vocal timbre, a too sudden change in the tempo of vocal rhythm was almost painful to me.

Clearly, there was a genetic contribution to my talents and to those of my siblings. While I became a composer, my sister Nina went on to become a successful concert pianist. My brother Laurence, who became an MD, played first trombone in the Florida all-state orchestra during his high school years, while our youngest sister, Mona, who became a lawyer and playwright, was also a talented pianist. My parents, for their part, not only enjoyed music but also had musical ability. My father had learned to play the violin as a child, possessed a beautiful tenor voice, and could sing arias by memory from various Italian operas. My mother, given her more difficult immigrant background, never had music lessons but she clearly enjoyed music and her children's active involvement.

My parents both came from Russian/Polish/Jewish backgrounds. In fact, my mother was born in Bialystok, Poland and brought to this country with her two little brothers when she was seven. Both my parents distinguished themselves academically, but because of the Great Depression my mother was unable to find a job in her chosen field of psychology. This may have factored into the timing of her marriage to my father, a promising young doctor.

Her early married life was beset with challenges, including her being left alone with two young children (I was eighteen months and my sister five months) for two and a half years while my father was posted to Italy and North Africa during WWII. Prior to his departure for Europe, my mother had moved around the country with him from army camp to army camp. It must have been an extremely arduous and anxiety-filled life for them. I still remember the excitement in May, 1945 when the war ended and I was carried into the streets in pajamas to see the celebration.

After my father returned home to Pearl River, a small town not far from New York City, he soon decided that he wanted to move to Texas. After that, we moved an additional four times. Throughout his life he was often dissatisfied, disgruntled, or frustrated in his professional life as a general practitioner, and later, radiologist. He often struggled financially. Why was his life as a gifted doctor so difficult and stressful? He was listed in *Who's Who in World Jewry*, *Who's Who in Jewish Men of Science*, and he published articles in major medical journals.

I believe the underlying reason for his recurrent professional turmoil and frustration lay in his difficult personality. As a specialist, he was dependent on referrals. For reasons I will never fully understand, it seems he did not get on well with other doctors. Looking back after these many years, I suspect my father may have been suffering from an undiagnosed bipolar disorder or some other serious psychiatric condition. In any case, it was apparent that his medical colleagues may not have liked him or did not want additional competition.

As a child, I experienced his angry outbursts and sometimes nasty treatment of my mother with pain and anxiety. My siblings and I felt powerless and sometimes frightened. We also had very little personal time with our mother who always worked, including several years as my father's x-ray technician. I missed her and often felt lonely for her company. She was so busy and exhausted that we children had to make appointments to see her in the evenings. On one occasion, my brother was scheduled first and when it was my turn to see her, she had already fallen asleep. I was terribly disappointed. It was only in my early forties that I began to understand how much I had missed her as a child. A short poem that I wrote at age thirteen conveys this sense of longing:

> I create
> in sad loveliness
> pictures
> of what it means
> to be forgotten
> by bees, butterflies,
> and lilies that grow –
> water freckles

The gift that emerged from this family drama was that I learned at an early age to create an inner world of my own. My deep enchantment with music fulfilled many emotional needs and provided a bulwark of continuity, security, and privacy, easing my loneliness as I created an imaginative world of sound and poetry. And while the many moves were initially quite upsetting to me, in retrospect I feel deeply grateful for the incredible artistic opportunities the changes of environment provided.

The first place I lived was Pearl River, New York. Despite its one hour proximity to the Big Apple, I hardly remember visiting the city. My parents' lives were too busy for such excursions, as my mother was taking care of three children under the age of six on the upper floor of the house while my father had his medical office on the lower floor. Still, my parents provided me with many opportunities. My first dance performance was in *The Nutcracker* when I was six years old. I had been taking ballet lessons for a year at a school two blocks from where we lived.

When I was seven, my father decided he wanted a change of locale. I did not understand why this disruption in my life had to occur, but my mother later explained that my father did not want to be "a big fish in a small pond." He was also expanding his practice as a general practitioner to include radiology, and thought that perhaps his breadth of training and expertise would be more valuable in another city. My mother tried to soften my resistance to being taken away from my familiar life and special attachments by saying that I would "learn a lot from new experiences and a new home elsewhere." "Love is better than learning," I replied.

We moved first to Brownwood, Texas and, a year later, to Dallas. It was in Brownwood that I began, at the age of seven, to take piano lessons from a sweet little old lady down the street, Miss Emma Johnson. My description of Miss Johnson is not a simple cliché. In fact she was sweet, little, and old. At eight and a half, my first creative attempts in composition occurred. Each week I became deeply engrossed in composing little piano pieces with fanciful names. Although I barely remember these childish efforts, I do remember my frustration when I couldn't make the pieces "come out" in a satisfactory way. Having no teacher or any technical knowledge of composition, I felt helpless and miserable when I got stuck. Eventually, my distress would precipitate a creative breakthrough and resolve the compositional dilemma. Even now, if I'm really having a hard time with a new piece, I can still feel temporarily helpless and miserable. But I no longer cry when this happens.

As I learned the piano repertoire and continued to compose, my young life took on new and magical dimensions. I began to search out biographies of the great composers in order to understand what they were like as children. "They had music in their heads and so do I," I thought. Clearly my preoccupation was quite different from that of many other little girls my age, whose major passion was horses.

A year later, we moved to the much larger city of Dallas. Here, thanks to my parents' generosity and support, I took ballet lessons in addition to continuing piano lessons. My teacher at the ballet school was none other than Alexandra Danilova of the Ballets Russes de Monte Carlo. As often happened with those great performers who left Europe because of the war and whose active dancing careers were fading, Danilova had become the star teacher in a major Dallas ballet academy. All her young students were in awe of her exotic Russian style, her elegance, discipline, and beauty. My little eight-year-old head was filled with excitement and wonder whenever this exotic creature appeared at our classes. I would dream about her and began to imagine choreographing my own dances with original music.

I had also begun to give public piano recitals with my sister Nina. My artistic world was expanding and I was very happy with and deeply attached to our life in Dallas. Thus, you can imagine my shock and displeasure when my parents announced that we would be moving to Florida in three weeks! To protest this rude shock, I ran away from home for a day. Of course I could not refuse to go, but I dug in my ten-year-old heels and did not speak for the entire trip.

This unwelcome move, first to Coral Gables and then to Miami Beach two years later, would again prove momentous and advantageous for my artistic growth. In Coral Gables, where we lived for one year, my sister Nina and I were often the featured pianists on our teacher's student recitals. And I continued to compose, this time organizing all the children on the block where we lived to perform in my little opera for which I had also created the libretto. (I was astonished when, about thirty years later, my father remembered the name of this ambitious project.) The production schedule for my opera was halted by our relocation to Miami Beach.

This newest move, however, resulted in a pivotal change in my musical life. I was now deeply aware of my needs as a very young composer who had never been trained. I told my mother that she must find a composition teacher for me — a piano teacher alone was insufficient.

Her efforts on my behalf brought into my life a mentor, Robert Strassburg, who would have a lifelong influence.

Again, an initially upsetting change in my life would prove fortuitous. To this day, I do not understand how a woman with four children, one of them a toddler, working herself to help support the family, and going through another major move, was able to find the one teacher in the greater Miami area who was perfect for me. My mother told me that when at twelve and a half I began studying with him, the light came into my eyes. At my mother's funeral in 2004, I spoke of my immeasurable gratitude to her for bringing him into my life at a critical period in my creative development.

I would study piano and composition with Mr. Strassburg for the next five years. An exceptional teacher, composer, conductor, musicologist, biblical scholar, and poet, he was not only a tremendous stimulus to my creative and intellectual growth, he also became a deeply nurturing and supportive presence. Regular lessons with him were the highlight of my week. Under his tutelage, my technical skill and my ability to deal with the occasionally chaotic rhythms of my creative process vastly improved. I learned to be more accepting of the anxiety and unease, as well as the exhilaration that are part of my compositional process. His extensive knowledge of literature, philosophy, and poetry was often brought into the conversation at appropriate moments during my lessons, and his large personal library was a source of great fascination. I was introduced to the Upanishads and the Vedas, the poetry of Bialik and Whitman, and the Psalms, several of which he encouraged me to use as texts in my first choral pieces.

Each week my mother drove my sister and me from Miami Beach to Coral Gables for our lessons. This long drive provided a very special time for us to be alone with our busy working mother. I still remember the rhyme on the twirling advertisement of the Mayflower Pancake and Donut House on Biscayne Boulevard that we passed every week:

> As you go through life, brother
> Whatever be your goal,
> Keep your eye upon the donut
> And not upon the hole

We lived in a beautiful house called Villa San Rafael in Miami Beach. With five bedrooms, four bathrooms, a fifteen by thirty foot living room, and a terrazzo-floored atrium, this house allowed us to practice at the same time — Nina upstairs, me downstairs — without hearing each other!

Nina and I gave many solo and duo-piano concerts throughout our high school years, performing a number of important works in the repertoire. One summer, just two weeks before we were scheduled to play the Mozart *Double Piano Concerto in E Flat Major*, Mr. Strassburg suggested I compose a cadenza. This was a daunting task but I accepted the challenge and finished the cadenza in time for our concert. In general, his approach was to give talented piano students demanding pieces that also provided a framework for his teaching of theory.

Under his mentorship, I was able, at the age of sixteen, to win a scholarship to the Junior Conservatory Camp in Vermont. This camp, which later became the Walden School, embodied the vision of Grace Cushman. A stellar musicianship and theory teacher at the Peabody Conservatory, Mrs. Cushman had created a unique summer program for young performers and composers. Students were selected from around the country to participate in classes and lessons while living in our "storybook castle," an old country house with seven gables and a turret.

Coming from Miami Beach to this idyllic New England setting was like entering a fairy tale. The most stimulating component of my magical summer was encountering the work of two young modern choreographers, Flora Cushman, a Limon dancer, and Georgia Cushman, a Graham dancer. I was soon invited to compose dance suites for their programs. Elated and intimidated at the same time, I found that the pressure of writing on very tight deadlines left me in a state of overdrive. Sometimes I was unable to sleep for an entire night, unable to turn the music off. (I am reminded of the 1948 film, *The Red Shoes*, where the soloist cannot stop dancing.) Nevertheless, the Junior Conservatory Camp, with its talented faculty and students, gave me my first experience of working collaboratively with gifted dancers and choreographers.

It also taught me how to compose quickly when required by a performance deadline.

Even though I had many interests and enjoyed various activities in high school – including varsity debating, languages, writing, and painting – Mr. Strassburg's deep understanding of my creative needs, his knowledge of many subjects, and his impish sense of humor made him the star teacher of my young life. Once, when I became quite defensive in response to his criticism of a new piece, he asked why I was so heated. I replied, "If I am not for myself, who will be for me?" Smiling in response, he said "I will." Thanks to his efforts in finding appropriate competitions for young composers, my compositions began to win prizes in local and national contests. He always had new creative projects to propose for me and, invariably, knew how to lift my spirits when dark adolescent moods clouded the horizon.

Why was such a remarkably gifted musician and scholar living in Coral Gables, Florida? Personal circumstances were the reason. His younger son had asthma and needed to live in a warm climate. Thus, this Harvard-educated and successful composer from New York City became a major professional presence in the greater Miami area. Bob belonged to the same generation as Lukas Foss and Leonard Bernstein, both of whom remained his lifelong friends. His career was hugely impacted by relocating from a major cultural metropolis to the relative backwater of southern Florida, and later, Los Angeles. Curiously, my move to Florida occurred after Bob had moved to Coral Gables from New York City and before he left Florida for California, where he spent many years as a distinguished professor at California State University in Los Angeles.

The guidance and presence of this superb mentor in my young life were immense gifts. Upon my graduation from high school, Bob gave me a book titled *The Wisdom of Israel* with the following inscription:

June 25, 1959

Dear Diane,

You are a delight
to my heart both for your
love of learning and for
the voice of music which will
always find resonance in
your inmost being

May your power to
move all hearts with
poetic sound grow with
the hours, days, and years.

Your teacher and
friend
Robert Strassburg

Letter from Robert Strassburg, 1959

𝄢:

Chapter Two

MY MUSICAL EDUCATION

Realizing how little I knew about the world of professional music and the daunting task of making a life as a composer, I decided that the best choice for my undergraduate education would be a major conservatory connected to a respected university. After consultation with my parents and Mr. Strassburg, I selected the Eastman School of Music. In 1959, at age seventeen, I left for Rochester. Here, I would spend four years (including more than a year at the University of Rochester), receive a Bachelor of Music in Composition with Distinction, and a Performer's Certificate in Piano, the highest undergraduate award a pianist can receive.

This last "pedigree" was almost an accident. Though not a piano major, I was assigned a major teacher since I had easily passed all the repertoire requirements for undergraduate piano major applicants. Luckily for me, I was assigned to Orazio Frugoni's studio. Frugoni, an unforgettable Italian, was unlike other members of the piano faculty at that time in his more flexible pedagogical style. Because I was a composition major, Frugoni gave me considerable freedom to choose difficult repertoire not generally known or taught then at this conservative musical institution. When I asked him if I could study the *Opus 11, Drei Klavierstücke* of Arnold Schoenberg, Stravinsky's *Piano Sonata* (1924) and *Sérénade en la*, and Mussorgsky's *Pictures at an Exhibition*, he agreed. In my senior year, Frugoni decided, as an afterthought, to enter me in a competition for the Performer's Certificate in Piano, normally restricted to outstanding piano majors. To my astonishment, I was awarded this prestigious diploma. Frugoni was enormously pleased and explained to me later that the entire piano faculty was in awe of anyone who could perform such difficult repertoire well and from memory, especially since they could not.

The Eastman School of Music, extremely conservative at that time, exposed me to a certain type of American conservatory training. The small and select student body, comprised of graduate and undergraduate students from all over the world, was immensely talented. As a neophyte in a professional milieu, I was intoxicated by my exposure to the stimulating artistic environment created by the Rochester Philharmonic, the variety of Eastman ensembles, and the superb orchestras and distinguished performers who visited the city. Besides taking a regular curriculum, I was immersed in a whirlwind of concerts, recitals, and competitions within the school itself. For the first time in my life, I had a community of talented friends who had comparable interests and ambitions. The performance resources for young composers were incredible. Even undergraduate composition majors often had their works read and performed by outstanding players and ensembles.

Summer studies also provided tremendous stimulus to my creative development. Each year I would apply for, and usually receive, scholarships to study with famous composers. During my first summer program, I spent five weeks in Darius Milhaud's class in Aspen, Colorado. The class was fairly large, about fifteen students, and included older composers such as Philip Glass and Joan Tower. I was scheduled to stay for the entire eight-week session but became deeply troubled about my music and wished to leave sooner. This inner crisis occurred because I was extremely self-critical and had decided I did not like my work. As the youngest participant in Milhaud's composition seminar, I may have been especially insecure about my music. To my surprise, Milhaud was most sensitive and solicitous. He told me that I was very talented and urged me to remain for the rest of the program. I was touched by his interest and concern, but still decided to leave early.

In addition to having serious doubts about the quality of my music, I had become conflicted about whether to continue my studies at the Eastman School or major in music at the University of Rochester. Many of the performance majors loved to practice five or six hours a day and were delighted by the minimal academic requirements at Eastman. However, I wanted more intellectual challenge than what was offered by the course requirements at Eastman and wondered if a more demanding liberal arts curriculum would be a better choice. I went through the formal process of application to the University of Rochester, was accepted, and spent the next year and a half finding out if "the grass was indeed greener."

Experience on a liberal arts campus gradually resolved my ambivalence. Yes, there were many more academic courses to choose from, but I had much less in common with the U of R undergraduate students than I did with the students at Eastman with whom I shared a clear life passion and direction. I decided to return to Eastman in order to have more time to concentrate on music during my junior and senior years.

During summers, I again studied with distinguished composers. In 1960, I went to the Inter American University of Puerto Rico in San German at the invitation of Roy Harris. Dr. Harris was unlike any teacher I had ever encountered. First, he demanded that all his students use his theory of tonality and write in his style. Although I found his criticisms of my music initially upsetting, I grew accustomed to his deconstructing every piece I brought to him and rewriting it to conform to his strict harmonic and tonal requirements. I would arrive for my daily lesson at his studio perched high on a hill near his home. Here, dressed in a long flowing velvet robe, Harris – a traditional, tonal composer – made biblical pronouncements on how the serialists were destroying western music. Too young to have crystallized my own position about this controversy, and too intimidated by his domineering personality, I did my best each week to fulfill his compositional demands. Although my compositions throughout the subsequent year continued to resemble his music stylistically, the enormous discipline he imposed on me was, in retrospect, quite useful.

13

In the summer of my junior year, I had the good fortune to study at Tanglewood, an international summer festival where renowned Polish composer Witold Lutoslawski was the primary guest composer. My entire experience of Tanglewood was immensely stimulating. I enjoyed the fun-loving and sophisticated European contingent, I was thrilled to sing in the Boston Symphony Chorale when Koussevitsky conducted Brahms' *Ein deutches Requiem*, and I had a pivotal introduction to the music of the Second Viennese School. I spent many hours in the Tanglewood library listening to works not performed or discussed at Eastman. New musical vistas were opening for me. When I complained to my teacher, Lukas Foss, how difficult it was for me to compose during that summer, he gave me sage advice: "Sometimes it is important to be creatively dormant as new seeds are being planted."

Returning to Eastman for my senior year, I was surprised to be called by the Woodrow Wilson Foundation for the purpose of arranging an interview with me. When I met with the Foundation panel in early winter, I was asked questions about the challenges of twentieth century music, what I thought about certain technical problems of musical syntax and structure, and my own aspirations as a composer. I do not remember exactly how I responded to these questions, except that I must have communicated to the three men, sitting at a table in the hotel conference room, a certain passion and confidence. To my astonishment, I received a letter from the Foundation several months later notifying me that I was the recipient of a Woodrow Wilson Fellowship.

How could this have happened? Normally, Eastman students were not eligible for such a fellowship. It seems that my checkered undergraduate career and adolescent conflict about a liberal arts versus professional music education had unexpected benefits. As a student at the University of Rochester, I had taken a highly-reputed undergraduate course given by well-known philosopher, Dr. Louis White Beck, an authority on Immanuel Kant. Evidently, Dr. Beck liked my papers and had given my name to the Woodrow Wilson Foundation two years later. Imagine that!

A funny and somewhat prescient event occurred at my Eastman graduation ceremony in 1963. Howard Hanson, the famous and rather conservative composer who was director of the school for many years, came over to congratulate me personally. I had never met Dr. Hanson, since he only taught graduate students. He was cordial and jovial, but then he said something that startled me. "Congratulations on your graduation from Eastman. I wish you much success, but I hope you won't write any of that terrible electronic music!"

His exhortation struck me like a bolt out of the blue. No electronic music program was available at Eastman in those years, and students were discouraged from pursuing such forbidden attractions. Furthermore, I was not one of the subversives in the school. I had no idea on that graduation day what a significant portion of my future creative life would be devoted to electronic and electroacoustic music. Nor could I have imagined the unlikely chain of events that would lead me to Princeton and introduce me to computer music five years later.

In October 1963, I married Joel Thome, a percussionist and conductor who, at age twenty-two, had become the youngest member of the Israel Philharmonic. We had met at Eastman when Joel was a senior and I was a freshman. Pursuing his courtship during our two-year separation, Joel phoned me from a ham radio in Lebanon during my Christmas break and offered me a *lavaliere*. I responded, "I'm not sure what a *lavaliere* is but, coming from you, Joel, I am sure it will be very nice."

Hanging up the phone, I was informed by my sister that accepting this beautiful pendant was a prelude to engagement. Since Joel and I had seen each other only briefly in the previous two years, first at Marlboro where he was performing, and later at Tanglewood, I decided to visit him in Israel after my graduation. That eight-week summer visit led to an engagement, which led to an October marriage and a year spent in Israel. I describe life with Joel in more detail in Chapter Five.

Suffice it to say, my adventurous change of personal plans and academic trajectory had major consequences for my professional future. A year later, the Woodrow Wilson Fellowship was indeed gone. Furthermore, Joel and I had decided to attend the University of Pennsylvania and study composition with George Rochberg, head of the music department. I would receive a Master of Arts degree in Theory and Composition from Penn and finish coursework for the PhD.

However, a new personal crisis was brewing. It was the late 1960s and the job market for college professors was dismal. In addition, Penn's track record in granting its doctoral degree was hardly encouraging. I began to question if I really wished to continue working towards a degree that would still not provide any assurance of employment.

In addition to my demoralized stance about Penn's academic program and the future job market, I was facing long and difficult retraining as a pianist. Unable to play without pain due to stretching a tendon in my right hand, I felt crippled. Every two weeks I traveled from Philadelphia to Brooklyn, New York to take lessons from a remarkable teacher, Dorothy Taubman. Mrs. Taubman specialized in retraining advanced pianists who had injuries. She was confident that, given time, she could make me a healthy pianist.

One day, on the train to the city for my lesson, I encountered an acquaintance married to a fellow Penn graduate student. She asked how I felt about my doctoral program at Penn. Mincing no words, I told her that I was extremely discouraged and unhappy. "Why don't you apply to Princeton?" she suggested. Though this idea had never occurred to me, I decided there was nothing to lose. I sent my portfolio, a list of recommendation names, and a completed application.

On April Fool's Day of 1968, I received a telegram from Princeton offering me a full fellowship for the next five years. Since I did not compose twelve-tone music, I was intimidated about which composition teacher to request. To my surprise, I was assigned to Milton Babbitt, the preeminent twelve-tone theorist and composer. I was greatly relieved when Mr. Babbitt turned out to be extremely approachable and charming. He was sincerely interested in my work and surprisingly non-dogmatic. One day he said, in his irrepressible manner, that he "didn't care if composers looked into the sunset for their ideas and inspiration."

He was immensely gregarious and loved to talk informally during my lessons before moving to compositional topics. Once, after telling me the story of a young male student who was deeply depressed and had committed suicide, he remarked, "Of course, a woman would not do such a thing since she could have children." "But, Mr. Babbitt," I replied, "a woman composer sufficiently depressed about her creative life might also commit suicide." I gradually began to realize that having a woman composition student was a novelty for Mr. Babbitt.

Throughout the five years of my studies, I lived in Philadelphia and traveled to Princeton for classes several days each week. I was constantly anxious about the quality of my academic work since Princeton gave no course grades. However, I found the intellectual climate very stimulating and I had a new compositional interest: computer synthesis. Research and creative exploration in this exciting area were then available at only two institutions: Stanford and Princeton. After several years of compositional experiments I completed my dissertation, which included a composition, *Polyvalence for Computer and Ensemble* and an analytical essay, *Toward Structural Characterization of the Timbral Domain.*

I received my PhD from Princeton in 1973, becoming the first woman to be granted such a degree in music. This distinction was due to the fact that Princeton had accepted very few women graduate students during that period. Little did I know that this fortuitous timing would catapult my professional life into an academic stratosphere. Throughout my Princeton studies, I had given little thought to the reality of eventually facing the academic job market. To my astonishment, the prestige of this degree made me a very desirable job prospect. I began to feel "like the pretty girl at the ball." Nevertheless, it would take several years and a major move before my life settled down personally, professionally, and geographically.

Chapter Three

AN ARTIST IN THE ACADEMY

As a graduate student at Princeton, I had lived in suspended time. At least, that's the way it felt. Immersed in an intellectual and creative bubble shared with a small coterie of other privileged denizens, I kept my nose to the proverbial grindstone. It took intense energy and focus to constantly learn new computer programs, prepare for oral and written exams, produce new creative work each year, and begin my dissertation.

The atmosphere was quietly competitive and it was impossible to be oblivious of the fact that I was one of two women graduate students. My trips to Princeton from Philadelphia were often shared with one other student who was also allowed to live off campus since we were both married and our spouses could not relocate. These trips were a source of occasional discomfort since my male chauvinist colleague often made gratuitous, semi-hostile remarks about women composers.

Throughout my studies at Princeton, I was also leading a parallel existence in Philadelphia. Joel had become director/conductor of the Philadelphia Composers' Forum, a major professional performing group for contemporary music. Our apartment served as an office, and we often entertained many visiting musicians and composers from the US and abroad. There was constant fundraising, grant writing, and meetings with the board, as well as concerts in Philadelphia and tours throughout the East Coast. I found this double life both exhilarating and exhausting. It also reminded me that composers had limited economic opportunities. While some composers chose to be active as conductors or performers, others formed collectives, worked in unrelated professions, or attempted to live off grants. The European model of state subsidy did not exist.

My choice was to support myself as a teacher, hopefully at a university. This decision was determined by an early awareness that my music would probably have little entertainment or commercial value. It was essentially art music. Knowing this, and having no doubt that such a rarefied and impractical specialty was my true direction, I imagined that an academic life in combination with a professional career made sense.

In later years, when the pressures of teaching felt overwhelming, I would sometimes envy those composers who lived from commission to commission or grant to grant. It was a helpful corrective for me to learn from some of these "in the world" types that such a life was far from ideal. In fact, successful composers applied for jobs at institutions where I was teaching. Once, when I was serving as co-chair of a National Endowment of the Arts composition panel, composer participants who were not academically affiliated commented on how fortunate I was. I returned to my ivory tower feeling very lucky indeed to have a good job. The American university now served as a twentieth century patron for art and artists.

But there was a price. One anecdote still brings a smile when it comes to mind. During the years of my graduate study at Princeton and parallel existence in Philadelphia, Joel and I often went to New York City to attend art exhibits, dance performances, and concerts. One evening we were invited to a party celebrating Joseph Machlis, the famous musicology professor whose new book had become a smashing commercial success. About seventy years old and still teaching, he quipped, "Academic life is wonderful if you can get through the first twenty-five years." Knowing looks were exchanged and laughter was heard throughout the room.

In 1974, I became an assistant professor at the State University of New York in Binghamton. This job, my first full-time academic position, proved to be an excellent experience in many ways. My teaching assignments included theory and twentieth century music classes, and I enjoyed the sophisticated and lively students, many of them from New York City. During the summers, when I did not teach, I raced to complete new works using a Moog analog studio for the first time. Coming from Princeton, I was only familiar with digital synthesis. Because my teaching schedule left little time for creative work, I had barely three months to learn to use an analog studio and finish a new piece.

To balance this somewhat hectic life, I took karate classes with a famous black belt instructor. Students were taught many *katas* (a specific series of forms) in his *dojo* (teaching studio), and had to pass strict tests before they could advance to the next level. It was here that I met two exceptional women with whom I became close friends. Of course, other mutual interests besides karate served to cement our friendship. Both women are outstanding violists: Judy became the first woman violist in the Philadelphia Orchestra; Evelina played with the St. Paul Chamber Orchestra in Minnesota for many years. Coincidentally, they are each multi-talented: Evelina is a published writer, Judy, an active painter. We have kept in touch for many years and sometimes enjoy bicoastal visits. I am still amazed that we initially met in karate class forty years ago. Getting to know them was a great antidote to my professional anxieties. So was practicing a new discipline, along with enjoying a totally different culture.

There was reason to feel anxious. As an untenured professor, I naturally had no secure future at the university. In fact, due to the politics within the department, the description of the position I held was being changed from that of composer to theorist. When it became clear that I would not remain on the faculty beyond June, 1977, I began to apply for jobs throughout the country.

Imagine my surprise in May, 1977, when the University of Washington in Seattle phoned to offer me a three year contract as an assistant professor. No interview was requested. Perhaps my multiple degrees in composition, theory, and piano, combined with a growing professional reputation, made the usual interview process unnecessary. I felt like a mail order bride. While I received job offers from other institutions, the University of Washington, a major research university with a large composition program and an active contemporary music group, seemed like the right choice. It was a momentous decision. I would be leaving everyone and everything I knew. I called Mr. Babbitt and asked his advice. "Diane, you would be a fool to turn down this job offer," he said.

I considered my professional options for a few weeks. Then, I remembered two enigmatic dreams I had had the previous month. In the first dream, which took place in my parents' New York apartment, my mother came to tell me that Veronica Boscovich, Uri's niece and a New York fashion designer, was on the phone and would like to speak to me. I replied that I could not take the call because I was "too tired." The next dream, which immediately followed was somewhat abstract and puzzling. Here I was standing out in the middle of a lake atop an incredible, very tall sculpture. People on the other side of the lake were waving, motioning that I should dive from this high structure and join them on their side of the lake. I wanted to dive but (I know this sounds silly) did not have my swim cap and felt frightened. At the close of the dream, I gathered my courage and plunged in, no swim cap.

These two premonitory dreams occurred a month before I received any job offers. When I actually faced the possibility of moving to the west coast, their meanings became transparent. The first dream could be interpreted as a farewell to my life with Joel, as represented by Uri's niece. Indeed I was tired of the stress that came with being married to an active conductor and juggling an intense double-career existence. (We had in fact been separated for several years.) I also wanted to live in a different environment than the high-powered, career-obsessed milieu of the Northeast. I was looking for a healthier balance between my inner and outer life, a balance that would allow me to cultivate other aspects of my being.

The second dream, which possessed a kind of archetypal beauty, illuminated and fulfilled the import of the first. It symbolized the big leap I would take in crossing from one shore to another and meeting friends on the other side. Even the sequence of these two dreams perfectly represented the path my life would now follow. The adventurous change of location from east to west in 1977 proved to be one of the most fortunate decisions of my life.

Having accepted the UW offer, I flew to Seattle on September 1, 1977. I was immediately captivated by its scenic beauty and the gorgeous coastal environment of Puget Sound. However, there was little time to enjoy the Emerald City, as I needed to get settled before classes began later that month. I first went to meet the director of the School of Music, who had offered me the job. "Where is your husband?" he asked. I replied that I was divorced. "We've all been divorced several times," he said, to which I responded, "Well, this is my first."

In a short time, I was introduced to the entire composition faculty. Not surprisingly, they were all men and relatively conservative composers. I soon learned from the chair of the department, William Bergsma, that they were not sympathetic to electronic music. I quickly decided that I would write only acoustic music for the next few years. This meant writing works for chamber ensemble, orchestra, chorus, and solo performers to reassure my male colleagues that I was entirely competent in the acoustic domain. Only after receiving tenure did I decide to return to the electronic medium.

For some years, I led a traditional musical life since the School of Music was in many ways a conservatory with the addition of theory, history, ethnomusicology, and composition departments. Appendix 3 is a reprint of a 2002 article from the *Seattle Times*, which sheds light on my relationship to the university and the larger community. At the same time, my professional life kept me connected to my own specialty, and my career continued to expand with commissions, recordings, and performances. I served on various national and international composer panels, including those in Washington, D.C., Portland, Oregon, Athens, Greece, and San Diego, California, and sometimes traveled to Europe for performances of my work. For example, I flew to Paris for a stellar performance of my piece *Silver Deer for violin and piano*, and traveled to London for performances of some of my electronic music.

Objectively, I realized how fortunate I was to be garnering increasing recognition in the professional world and to be teaching at a major university. There was a price however. Unlike the performance faculty, whose duties were largely confined to giving their students private lessons, the composition faculty taught a variety of undergraduate and graduate classes. The UW was on the quarter system and, at that time, assistant professors in the theory/composition program were assigned to teach three courses each quarter. In the first five years alone, I taught a gamut of subjects, including *Modal and Tonal Counterpoint*, *History of Theory*, multiple different level theory courses, and a wide variety of analysis courses. In addition to teaching academic subjects, I gave weekly composition lessons. Since private lessons were not counted as part of the teaching load, the schedule was particularly demanding. All composers carried this dual pedagogical responsibility, although senior faculty had smaller course loads in addition to their private composition students. Composers Lab, an open course for all composition majors and composition faculty, was also held every Friday. Besides weekly meetings of the entire faculty, the theory/composition department convened frequently to monitor and evaluate a comprehensive theory program, which served the entire School of Music. Inundated by meetings, classes, and course preparations, I began to understand why many composers could not tolerate such an unrelenting schedule and remain creatively active.

And yet creative output was also a requirement for academic advancement. The professional life of a UW composer spanned several domains: teacher, creator, and entrepreneur. To advance in the academic hierarchy, all faculty members had to demonstrate evidence of publication or other forms of career recognition. Accomplishment in one's field was especially critical for assistant professors, since the granting of tenure at a major research university requires proof of excellence in research, as well as teaching and service. Not only did composers have to create music and get it published and recorded, they also needed to have their works presented around the country and the world. Building and sustaining a public reputation while simultaneously supervising doctoral students, giving private composition lessons, and teaching a huge array of academic subjects, made "publish or perish" a complicated and daunting endeavor.

One evening, I met Frank Guarerra, a senior colleague, during the intermission of a School of Music concert. A retired opera singer with a major career behind him, he was now enjoying life as a voice teacher.

"How are things going?" was his friendly inquiry. "Everything's fine," I replied "but I am *so* tired." He responded with a smile, "Still, it's a good job." Years later, as chair of the composition program, I would sometimes humor my exhausted junior colleagues when they came to my office for comfort and advice. "Remember, if we don't want the job, there are two hundred composers who do," I would say.

Not long after I arrived in Seattle, my career received an unexpected boost in the form of a telegram from Oklahoma. The physics department at the University of Tulsa had organized an unusual music festival in which my work had been programmed. Knowing that the local audience would have little interest in electronic repertoire, the organizers decided to concurrently celebrate the 75th birthday of Aaron Copland. The governor, the mayor, and other local dignitaries were in the audience on opening night, featuring a concert of Copland's music. This Trojan horse strategy, which had raised sufficient funds for the entire festival, was responsible for my first important recording. *Los Nombres, for computer, percussion, and piano* was released in 1978 on an album titled *New Directions in Music.*

In addition to performing and recording while in Oklahoma, I also had the pleasure of meeting Aaron Copland. Staying at the same charming hotel, we met at breakfast on the verandah one morning. Copland began to ask about my compositional background. To my astonishment, as soon as I mentioned Princeton and Milton Babbitt, he went into a ferocious tirade against twelve-tone composers. I suddenly realized that, no matter how secure his reputation, he still harbored a deep competitiveness toward other composers. This was not the last time I would hear one artistic icon rail against another, or apparently suffer from the competitiveness of professional life. I saw firsthand how distressing an egoistic identification with one's career could become. While it is natural for artists to be identified with their work, I remembered these wise words of Lao Tsu, the ancient Chinese philosopher. They expressed an important lesson for me: "Just remain at the center, watching. And then forget that you are there."

My professional horizons continued to expand as I received commissions and performances over the next thirty years, and had a number of works recorded by major ensembles and soloists. Later in this memoir, I provide selected program notes, which give information about certain pieces and how they came to be written. However, to give a fuller portrayal of my public life and some of its delightful surprises, I will describe several experiences.

The first occurred when a concert of my music was given at the Collège Claude Debussy at the École Nationale de Musique de Danse et d'Art Dramatique in Saint Germain-en-Laye, France. This event, unusual for a young American composer, took place thanks to the efforts of an outstanding French violin/piano duo, Adele Auriole and Bernard Fauchet. We had met a few years earlier when they were touring in the United States. As specialists in contemporary music, they were interested in my work and suggested I let them know when I would visit Europe. Having been invited by noted composer Jonathan Harvey and other British colleagues to present my music at their universities during one of my spring breaks, I wrote to Bernard and Adele. They arranged a program to follow my residencies in England, and I came to France a few days later to attend the rehearsals and concert.

A big surprise happened one afternoon as we were driving to the hall where Bernard would premiere my solo piano piece, *Pianismus*. He had mentioned casually that we would make a stop at the French radio studio to say a few words about the concert. What he did not mention, until we were in the car, is that I would be speaking in French! My rusty language skills somehow managed to get me through this potentially embarrassing situation. Perhaps Bernard was more of a tease than I knew. In any case, chatting informally with the interviewer, we pulled it off.

American composers generally belong to either ASCAP or BMI, the two major performance rights organizations that collect royalties on behalf of their members. I had become friends with James Roy, head of BMI Concert Music Administration, when he visited Seattle during a national Society of Composers Conference that I had organized in 1982. A champion of American contemporary music and its dissemination in Europe, James had arranged a meeting between his London colleague and myself during another trip to Europe. As we drove in a taxi to the restaurant where my elegant host was taking me for lunch, something amusingly relevant occurred. Traffic came to a dead stop and we waited for the obviously important entourage to pass. "What is all the commotion about? " I asked. "Dolly Parton is in town," he responded, "and she's one of BMI's most successful members." I felt very grateful to Dolly as I realized it was the huge earning capacity of such popular stars that made possible the support BMI gave to composers such as me. Besides, I like Dolly.

The story of how and where I received news about my tenure will conclude this chapter. Like most assistant professors, I went through a long and anxious review process, never feeling certain of the outcome. Compounding my uneasiness, the university went through a major budget crisis that could easily have resulted in the removal of my position. As the tenure clock approached midnight, I fulfilled all the review requirements. These included dossiers galore documenting my professional accomplishments, teaching excellence, university and national service, as well as recommendations from sources both known and unknown to me.

Again, my personal life enters the picture. My companion during this period was a well-known political scientist whose specialty was Indian politics. A full professor, he was on sabbatical leave during part of our relationship. During my winter academic break, I joined him in New Delhi where I had a privileged and memorable exposure to an incredible culture. The director of the School of Music, an ethnomusicologist married to an Indian, also happened to be in New Delhi at the same time. On New Year's Eve, we were all enjoying a wonderful holiday party at the Delhi International Center. Just before the champagne was opened, the director came over and whispered in my ear: "Your tenure has been granted with a unanimous vote by the College Council and unanimous, minus one, from the School of Music." This news, music to my ears, was the best New Year present I could have received!

My maternal grandparents, New York City, 1930

My mother, Nina, and me – New York, 1945

At my home in Lake Forest Park, 1985

Chapter Four

THE GENDER ISSUE

(YES, IT WAS AN ISSUE)

Chauvinism and sexism so deeply pervaded the culture in which I was raised that I took these realities for granted. At the same time, my natural rebelliousness made me wish to create an independent life. Because I had different interests and goals compared to other children my age, I often felt like a loner, and while I enjoyed friendships, parties, debating society matches, and other high school activities, I was not comfortable with the hyper-sophisticated social environment of Miami Beach.

Family dynamics provided additional fuel for my sense of alienation. Although my parents were responsible and generous in providing educational opportunities for their four children, I found their relationship distressing. My mother, extremely bright and well-educated, was a woman of her generation and background. After she graduated from Hunter College with high honors in history, French, and geology, she was unable to find a satisfying job. When she married my father, her life was irrevocably changed, and while she worked in various jobs throughout her marriage, returning to her own field of psychology only in her fifties, she remained a traditional and subservient wife. My father, for his part, was not only temperamentally difficult and unpredictable, but also authoritarian and chauvinistic in his treatment of the entire family.

While I may have wished for a warm, fuzzy, protective daddy like some of my friends had, living with a very intelligent father who was hardly a pussycat was a useful rehearsal for the highly competitive and male-dominated profession I would enter. Meeting a number of world-famous male composers (they were the only composers who were famous during my generation) was hardly intimidating after growing up with Daddy.

In previous chapters, I have alluded to various situations where gender and/or gender bias clearly played a role. In fact, I have had a multitude of professional and personal experiences in which sexism, involving women as well as men, was evident. I found some of these experiences shocking and distressing; others I accepted as "par for the course." A pivotal illustration of the former happened during my graduate student years at the University of Pennsylvania. In Chapter Two, I did not explain a primary reason for my demoralization with the doctoral program at Penn. This is quite a story! To put it in a nutshell, I was summarily kicked out of school at the whim of the composition chair, George Rochberg. Two months later, I was reinstated by a unanimous vote of the full faculty.

The initial shock came when I received a letter from George informing me that I would be suspended permanently from the program for reasons of "unsatisfactory academic performance." I was stunned. Having been at Penn for three years, I had already received the Master of Arts degree, been admitted into their doctoral program, won composition prizes within and outside of the school, and maintained a consistently high grade point average. If my academic performance was unsatisfactory or inadequate, why had no one informed me?

In tears, I called George and asked him the reason for the abrupt decision regarding one of his "favorite students." "Diane," he replied in a patronizing voice, "I don't think you have the intellectual grip. Someday, you will thank me for this."

I was dumbfounded, devastated, hurt, and angry. Deciding to fight what appeared to be a capricious and unilateral action, I wrote a letter to the entire music faculty asking to be reinstated. The letter documented my well-received course work, including comments on my papers from various professors. It gave a summary of my creative productivity and showed that I had completed the extensive language requirements. I asked the faculty to consider reinstating me on the basis of an excellent academic record. Several weeks later, I was reinstated.

Why did such a blatantly sexist event occur? Ruminating about this question, I concluded that it probably had something to do with a too close personal relationship with George and Gene Rochberg. A month before I received the letter of dismissal, Joel and I had invited George and Gene to a party with close friends of ours in New Jersey. The party had particular interest for George because some well-known and influential artists from New York would be there. Relaxing into the party atmosphere, I participated as an equal in sharing my artistic opinions with others around the lively dinner table. I probably did not behave like a diffident student in that moment. George's possible anger with me, following that evening, was the only way I could make sense out of his humiliating treatment several weeks later. Truly, I will never know what went on in his mind. However, my sense of utter betrayal by a previously supportive mentor paved the way for my going to Princeton.

While I could describe many instances of sexism throughout my professional life, I will mention just a few. One anecdote comes to mind when I recall my first national computer music conference. Hosted by the University of Illinois in 1972, the conference included about two hundred men and two women. I was especially excited to participate since one of my pieces was programmed. Like other attendees whose works had been selected, I was invited to a late evening reception at the home of the organizer. When I arrived, the well-known individual hosting the party did not look at me or say a word of greeting. Not knowing anyone, and noticing that no male composer seemed to be interested in conversing with me, I went into the kitchen and had a friendly visit with the host's wife. This story illustrates a common characteristic of many male composers in this period. They were often unaccustomed to dealing with women outside of certain conventional roles. This reality is also portrayed in my next reminiscence.

The departmental faculty I joined at the UW was comprised entirely of men, eight to be precise. With one exception, they all belonged to an older generation. Thanks to new laws prohibiting gender discrimination, the gradual opening of academic positions to qualified women was in effect. After serious scrutiny, my future colleagues had chosen me as their first woman member. This proved to be a new experience for everyone. I soon realized that having me in their midst was a big adjustment, both socially and academically. They were not accustomed to having women as their professional peers.

Throughout my studies, I was usually the only woman composition student in a class of men, or the only female private student of a male teacher. However, I had no experience of teaching women composition students until I came to the University of Washington. During my second year on the faculty, we admitted two very talented young women composers into the graduate program, and they selected me as their teacher. These two were no shrinking violets. One, in particular, was a dramatically attired lesbian. I quietly observed that some of my colleagues were not entirely comfortable when she began her degree program.

Some amazing changes took place in their attitudes, though, as my two students pursued their studies. It gradually became apparent that they were exceptionally talented performers, as well as excellent composers. One was a gifted conductor who often presented music of her fellow students at the Composers Lab concerts. The other was an outstanding singer whose talent was of great benefit to her fellow students. These young women were gradually recognized as two of the most outstanding composers in our program, consistently winning annual school awards voted on by the departmental faculty. The ice had been broken.

During the 1980s, there were more festivals and conferences devoted exclusively to music by women. I rarely attended these, since I had limited opportunity for professional travel, which required brief absences from teaching. Also, I needed to focus on national or international performances of my work. However, I had a truly novel experience at a regional conference in 1986, when I attended a Women's Conductor and Composer Symposium in Eugene, Oregon. Extremely curious about the music and the conference topics, I encountered an environment charged with political excitement. Immediately I noticed that, instead of being an isolated woman at a conference of men, I was now part of a tiny minority of non-gay women. How interesting! What was not so interesting was the music itself. Very few of the concert programs had pieces that I found compelling. In some cases, political texts of vocal works were the major compositional element. Lack of technical skill permeated certain pieces; in others, the music seemed unimaginative. I came away from the long weekend disappointed in the artistic level of the programming, and somewhat less sympathetic to the obvious political motivation of the conference. For me, the best takeaway from a contemporary music festival is always the discovery of a wonderful new piece.

It has been said that one measure of gender (or other) equality has been reached when mediocrity is democratic. This means that, to be successful, women composers need be no more talented than their male counterparts. In my experience, this was not what usually happened. The statistical imbalance of concert programs that include music by women is well known. It is worth noting that, when music by women is selected, it is often of higher quality than that of their male counterparts. In other words, the starting line is different. Since it is generally rare to hear truly original or impressive new work, I was delighted when the best pieces on many festivals were composed by the tiny minority of women whose music had been programmed.

This was especially true in the brave new world of electronic and computer music. To help address organizational sexism, and because I was a respected composer, the International Computer Music Association invited me to curate a CD of new compositions. Attending an International Computer Music Conference in Greece during the mid-90s, I was enjoying a leisurely lunch in Athens with a male colleague who served on the board. I was quite surprised when he asked me to be the next curator. "Why would the organization choose such a critical, even unsympathetic, listener? I don't even like most of this music," was my blunt response. "That's exactly why we are asking you," he replied. After careful research, I selected five pieces from composers around the world. Three were by women, including younger women.

To give a somewhat fuller picture of my professional experience in a man's world, it was often male colleagues who gave me generous encouragement. Over the years I received many comments, letters, and emails expressing tremendous enthusiasm about my work and urging me to keep writing music. These encouraging and unexpected communications meant a great deal to me, since it was easy to feel uncomfortable and alienated when a particular male colleague expressed envy or hostility. It always helped to remind myself of the enormous support I had received from my composition teachers, all of them men, beginning with Robert Strassburg. It also helped that, during thirty-five years of attending festivals and conferences, I witnessed increasing numbers of women becoming active and successful composers. What helped most was my awareness that the vast majority of women in the world often experience lives of great suffering and have little personal freedom or control over their destinies. I realized that I enjoyed, and continue to enjoy, an incredibly fortunate and privileged life.

This last statement brings me back to the larger issue of discrimination facing women. Obviously, women artists are a subset of women in society. In recent years, there have been huge paradigmatic shifts in the relation of gender to the cultural landscape. This has come about through the ongoing work of outstanding feminist theorists and historians, the inclusion of Women's Studies programs in many college curricula, the activism of various national and international organizations that promote the work of women, and other such initiatives. Of course, major changes in the law and in social conventions have been hugely influential. While these positive changes are important and gratifying, sexism and gender discrimination in the profession have certainly not disappeared.

In the early 1980s, along with many others, I received a questionnaire about the experiences of women composers from composer/theorist Elaine Barkin. Our responses were published in "Perspectives of New Music," a widely read professional publication. Rereading my letter after many years, I am struck by how closely it corresponds with my present outlook.

Dear Elaine,

*I found your questionnaire interesting and sometimes difficult
to address with specific replies. It is easy enough to respond
to certain points, e.g., yes, I have been asked by males why I
don't have babies like normal women; why I compose at all
since a biological outlet for my creativity exists. I have been
accused of neglecting my man for my work, and I have felt
angry, frustrated, appalled by a variety of chauvinistic remarks
made over the years by men in various spheres of my life. I
could answer some other questions, those that fall into the
categories of personal history or predilection, without delay or
dilemma. However, what I find more provocative are some
other issues triggered in my mind by this forest of queries.*

*I do believe that serious composers are a particularly
individualistic-minded group beset with massive public
relations problems vis-à-vis the society as a whole. One thing
that makes being a woman composer sometimes more difficult
is that the socialization of women is far more supportive of
relationship as a primary goal in their lives than it is of inner,
solitary, artistic/intellectual pursuit. Thus, the part of her that
is deeply creative and artistically aspiring is brought into
real conflict with that part of her which is influenced by, and
identified with, her background, history, environment. I do not
think that men experience such conflicts to the same degree.*

*Also reflective of the general fallout from their socialization
are the ways in which women deal with their creative process.
I believe that they are more willing to view the compositional
act in emotional as well as intellectual terms, and to discuss
it more personally and more intimately. My experience with
male and female students has supported this statement.*

You ask, why is there a plethora of women's group activities? This is certainly a response to the factual and felt discrimination in the way women and their works have been dealt with. No doubt, there are also other reasons behind this phenomenon, including the gender politicization of almost all professional activity in the light of our rising individual and collective consciousness.

Finally, I cannot help feeling a keen schism at times between the composer, who is a more generalized and abstract part of myself, and the woman, who is daily aware of, and made aware of, what it means to be a woman and a composer. I do believe that, for all the ambiguity and complexity which impact this double identity, it is possible and necessary to separate the two. A composer is a composer. Given more supportive, less thwarting and hostile, less internally divisive environments, I am fully convinced that the history of women's creativity would have been on a par with men's.

Sincerely,
Diane Thome

Chapter Five

COMPOSING A LIFE

I have included this chapter in my memoir because it is truly impossible to separate my professional and personal lives. They have overlapped and intertwined with each other for almost half a century. Moreover, the great loves and deep friendships I have experienced have immeasurably enriched my creative development. The multiple currents flowing throughout my life suggest that I was both consciously and unconsciously attempting to integrate my external world with different facets of myself. Continuing this process of discovery and integration, I find it useful to pause and reflect on my journey thus far.

Several distinct threads provide a framework for various aspects of this journey. What unifies these threads is the central role of love. By this I mean not only romantic love and friendship, although this plays an important part, but also my love for works of art, music, poetry, and philosophy. The first and most obvious thread, underpinning the others, is my passion for music. As a young musician, I often fell in love with pieces of music, which I heard in my head for months at a time. This experience is not surprising, since young writers, painters, scientists, and mathematicians also find connection and exhilaration when they first encounter works of art or theory that have unique attraction for them. Not only did the piano repertoire captivate me, especially pieces by Beethoven, Chopin, and Schumann, I was also deeply affected by such larger works as Bach's *B Minor Mass* and Mozart's *Requiem*.

Besides walking around with my own compositions in my head, I could instantly access a private classical jukebox long before iPods and other such devices were available.

In my early teens, I was exposed to great literature and philosophy in various traditions. These included Sufi poetry, the Upanishads and Vedas of ancient India, the Psalms of the Old Testament, and the writings of the American Transcendentalists. Such intellectual interests also had a huge emotional component for me. Besides enlarging my world, as all great literature does, particularly inspiring literary works often enabled me to center and guide my inner life. Later, some of these writings played a significant creative role when I needed texts that had a special resonance for me. In addition, they pointed me in the direction of another enduring love, namely, a quest for spirit or soul. I will write more about this later.

It may appear that I was so absorbed by creative and intellectual life that I had little interest in, or time for, a normal teenage existence. This is not entirely true. I could throw myself into a whirlwind of social activity with great pleasure, but only for limited periods of time. Then I would withdraw into solitary pursuits. I needed to maintain a delicate balance between the introvert and extrovert parts of my make-up. Growing up in mid-1950's Miami Beach, I felt like an outsider. I witnessed the hotbed party atmosphere in the land of Miss Universe contests with a mixture of curiosity, discomfort, and detachment. But I also benefitted from the sophisticated social education this environment provided. Unease within the family, combined with a sense of alienation from the prevailing values of the culture, probably accelerated my individuation process.

Although I enjoyed dances and parties (even winning a mambo contest when I was fifteen), my teenage outlook did not include high expectations for a romantic life. Not only did I not believe in "someday the prince will come," I was not sure that I would be interested in creating a life with the prince, nor he with me. Given this unhopeful early perspective, it is a great irony that I have had a magical love life. To be candid, more than one prince came.

Unlike some women composers who chose partners with no artistic or professional interests similar to their own, I married two men who were both stimulating and invaluable to my creative development. In fact, it would have been inconceivable for me, as a young woman, to imagine marrying at all unless I felt deeply understood as an artist. The unique understanding and companionship, as well as the love that I received in both my marriages, still provide deep bonds of friendship with my two former husbands.

Even my first teenage romance developed because of shared artistic values. As a fifteen-year-old, I had not shown much interest in boys. My sister Nina, however, a year younger than me, was far more sophisticated socially. One day, she and her boyfriend Mel decided that it was time that I had a romantic interest in my life. I must say, Nina and Mel made a very appropriate choice in the person of a young man from New York City who came down to Miami Beach every summer with his parents. Julian was already in college at Columbia University and, most significantly, he was director of the classical music station. Of course, Julian was quite pleased to have a new girlfriend who was a pianist and composer. The fact that we lived in different cities only seemed to intensify our interest in each other. In addition to exchanging letters throughout our separations, we were able to meet at least once during the academic year since Nina and I would visit relatives in New York. I can still remember Julian's mother preparing lunch for us to eat in his bedroom as we listened to music. She was very purposeful, if not exactly subtle, in bringing us multiple courses, which required that the bedroom door was left continuously open to her eagle eye.

This was my first true romance, and it is even possible that it might have developed into a more mature and serious relationship were it not for a significant change in my life. Graduating from Miami Beach High School when I was seventeen, I had decided to go to a professional music school and had chosen the Eastman School in Rochester, New York. Coming out of a traditional religious background, I decided that if I wanted to date, I should meet Jewish boys. One evening, I attended a meeting of Eastman's Hillel Association. As I quickly discovered, the charming, blond, blue-eyed president of Hillel was Joel

Thome. Moreover, he was a gifted percussionist and conductor. When the percussion department announced a competition for new works for ensemble, I entered a composition and won the contest. This brought me into even greater contact with Joel, who conducted the percussion ensemble. Soon, a relationship began to blossom. At this point, I realized that I needed to make a choice between Julian, with whom I was still in contact, and Joel. The decision favored Joel, whose personality, interests, and temperament seemed far more compatible with my own.

As our relationship continued to develop, I started to feel uneasy about the asymmetry of our feelings for one another. Joel, three years older and far more mature, had become increasingly serious about our possible future together. On the other hand, I was not ready to make such a commitment and needed to make a break. When my girlfriends found out that I had made this change, they informed me that I was crazy. Joel was very popular, to say the least. Meanwhile a major move was about to take place in Joel's life. Carlo Maria Giulini, then conductor of the Israel Philharmonic Orchestra (IPO), was visiting Eastman and auditioning musicians. As a result, Joel was invited to join the IPO and became its youngest member when he was twenty-two. Leaving his graduate studies at Eastman and moving to Israel, he now pursued a long distance courtship, including phone calls from a ham radio station in Lebanon.

Except for our brief meeting at Tanglewood where I was a summer student, I did not see Joel for the next two years. Meanwhile, to encourage this long distance romance, even my piano teacher, Orazio Frugoni, who was a friend of Joel's, got involved, bringing travel brochures for Israel to my lessons. Having received the beautiful *lavaliere* from Joel's parents when they visited Rochester, I realized that I was practically engaged to a man I had seen only once in two years. I decided it was time to bite the bullet and visit Joel in Israel. Having saved up $500 from various jobs, I could now buy myself a KLM Royal Dutch Airlines ticket to Tel-Aviv, treating myself to a very special graduation present from Eastman.

I spent the next eight weeks in a whirlwind of marvelous vacation activities. Joel had arranged for me to stay in the lovely apartment of

Mrs. Routberg. A gracious lady in her sixties, Mrs. Routberg spoke no English and I spoke no Hebrew, so we communicated in French. In fact Mrs. Routberg began to read French love poetry to me as she became more aware of the nature of our relationship. Each morning, Joel would drive up in his little white Renault and we would take trips to different parts of Israel, including Haifa, Jerusalem, Tiberias, Masada, Eilat and other places. For a young woman who had never traveled beyond the United States, I found these excursions truly fascinating. Having lived in Israel for several years, Joel was a great tour guide.

An additional component of my stay in Israel was my introduction to Joel's friends and colleagues, among them major artists in the country. These included Yemenite Jews from the Israel Dance Theatre such as Margalit Oved, premiere dancer; Alec Spielman from Jerusalem, a former violinist and Israeli spy who gave us yoga lessons; and Hannah Brand, a retired Hungarian opera singer and wonderful gracious lady who had survived the Holocaust. Most important, Joel introduced me to his closest friend and mentor, Alexander Uriah Boscovich. "Uri" was a Hungarian composer whose life had been saved during WWII only because he was unable to return to Europe after a performance of his music by the Israel Philharmonic when he was a very young man. Over time, he became an esteemed composer, teacher, and critic. It was his influence that motivated Joel to become a composer.

I too became a devoted student, finding Uri's ideas about musical structure very original and compelling. Our relationship went further: Joel and I were essentially members of the family. Uri's wife, Miriam, was an active pianist, also on the faculty of the Tel-Aviv Conservatory, and their two young children, David and Sarit, adored Joel. We often went on excursions with the whole family and enjoyed many wonderful evenings at the Boscovich home where well-known artists were frequently invited.

At the end of an idyllic summer during which we became engaged in Jerusalem, we married in New York City, and spent our first year together in Israel. I was essentially forfeiting the Woodrow Wilson Fellowship that awaited me in the States. Such a decision might have seemed a bit romantic, and indeed it was. Nevertheless, our year in

Israel was tremendously happy and rewarding. Joel continued his activities as percussionist and conductor and I became studio pianist for the Israel Dance Theatre. Of course we remained Uri's devoted composition students throughout the year. Shortly before returning to the United States for graduate school, we took Uri to the hospital. It was a terribly sad day for us knowing that we would never see him again. He died of lung cancer at the age of fifty-three, having influenced an entire generation of young composers.

What I wish to emphasize here is that this shared life opened an incredibly interesting and illuminating door to a world I would probably not have encountered were it not for Joel. When we traveled in Europe, for example, we were invited to dinner at Karlheinz Stockhausen's home in Cologne, Germany. I still remember the delicious fruit soup prepared by his Silesian housekeeper and talking until midnight with this eminent composer about art, philosophy, and spiritual ideas. In another instance, when Joel was accepted to a summer conductor's workshop led by Pierre Boulez, we went to Basel, Switzerland for three weeks. I enrolled as an auditor and had the rare privilege of hearing truly masterful interpretations of the music of Schoenberg, Berg, and Webern for the first time. It was very inspiring. It was also tremendous fun to attend the gala party hosted by Boulez when the workshop and concerts ended.

Our circle of friends in New York City included sculptors, painters, composers, actors, and choreographers. One special friend was Lillian Kiesler, widow of the Bauhaus architect and designer, Friedrich Kiesler. I have a beautiful water color painting given me by Lillian, who also acted in many avant-garde theatre works of director Robert Wilson. A wonderful and supportive friend, this colorful, effervescent woman died in her early nineties after years of archival and museum work on behalf of Kiesler, in addition to her painting and acting. Lillian's energetic spirit and delightful humor through her later years remain an inspiration.

Another very important friend was choreographer Anna Sokolow. Anna had founded her own company, which became quite famous and successful. We often attended performances of her work in New York and enjoyed many special private visits. We gradually began to understand how difficult it was to run a company and how competitive the dance world was. Anna faced many struggles, both internal and external. We slowly realized that her close friendship with us was a source of comfort and pleasure to her. The opportunity of knowing a number of distinguished senior artists, all of whom had lived exciting and fulfilling lives, was a tremendous privilege for us.

Living in Philadelphia, we soon began to follow divergent career paths. I worked on my master's and doctoral degrees at the University of Pennsylvania while Joel, realizing that he was more interested in a professional career than an academic one, founded the Philadelphia Composers' Forum. Over the next few years this organization developed a reputation as one of the most outstanding and successful contemporary music ensembles in the country. Its members came from all over the East Coast and its repertoire included music by both European and American composers. Joel was an innovative and charismatic music director/conductor and, over the years, recordings and residencies as well as concerts became part of the season's calendar.

While I found this whirlwind of activity, in which I too was involved, both exciting and stimulating, it left little time for personal life. In addition, I was experiencing various strains as a graduate student and injured pianist, which I describe in Chapter Two. I finally did leave Penn for Princeton in 1968, finishing my PhD in 1973. At that point I was offered a job in upstate New York at the State University of New York in Binghamton. By this time, various strains in my marriage induced me to separate from Joel. While we kept in touch, the marriage, for me, was over and eventually we divorced. Nevertheless, the rich experiences we shared created a lasting bond. For eleven years we were united not only personally, but also in bringing contemporary music to a wider audience and in knowing a world of remarkable and talented people.

During the first year in my new surroundings in upstate New York, an amazing event took place. Unexpectedly, I fell head over heels in love! The man involved was an ebullient Russian with a sonorous bass speaking voice and a wonderful sense of humor. We met through a mutual friend in New Jersey who happened to be a well-known astrologer.

When Sylvia learned that I would be moving to Binghamton, she said that I must meet her friend Nick.

One day while I was working in my office, the phone rang. When I picked it up, a man with a deep Russian voice introduced himself as Sylvia's friend and suggested that he show me around Binghamton. Over the next few weeks of dating, astonishment took over as I realized that we were simply "crazy about each other." Being somewhat cautious and reserved in matters of the heart, I was utterly amazed about this state of tremendous happiness permeating my life. This development was especially surprising since Nick and I lived in two different worlds, Nick as an entrepreneur and international businessman and I as a composer and academic. Nevertheless, we seemed to magically "click."

I found his life story almost miraculous. As a youth, he had nearly starved to death when the Germans invaded Russia during WWII. After the war, he and his mother managed to immigrate to the United States where he entered engineering school. Over time he became a very successful businessman. Nick's ebullience, energy, and charm were captivating, especially given the earlier struggles and traumas in life that he had overcome. I was full of admiration. Besides, he was also tremendous fun to be with!

Over the next three years our love affair continued, enriched by winter vacations in Aruba, a Caribbean island where Nick owned property, and countless wonderful evenings of dinner and dancing. Nick's presence was certainly a very bright light in my life in Binghamton. Inevitably, however, the relationship would come to an end when I had to leave Binghamton because I needed a job. As a young assistant professor without tenure, I was teaching in a very small music department where nasty politics and no certainty of continued employment were in the air. I resolved that in the future I should join a larger faculty.

There was really nothing we could do to sustain our relationship since Nick, given his business commitments in New York State, was not prepared to relocate and I was determined to continue my professional life on the West Coast. "You might as well go to the end of the world," he said when I explained what was happening. Nevertheless, the thought of our time together many years ago still makes me smile.

When I left the East Coast for Seattle in 1977, my biggest fear was that I would lose connection with the deepest relationships of my life thus far. Fortunately, this fear proved to be unfounded. I remain connected, more than ever, to those special individuals who shaped and enriched my life, wherever they may be. And needless to say, in Seattle I made wonderful new connections.

Having become better acquainted with the School of Music faculty, I had frequent conversations with Alberto, a Cuban pianist who also had a background in architecture and the visual arts. One day I asked him, "Alberto, do you know any local painters or artists? I would like to meet people outside of music since I have always had friends in other fields."

"Yes," he answered, and soon introduced me to his friend, Maxine. I was very appreciative of this new association and enjoyed getting to know Maxine and her work, especially her original installations. As with many artists, Maxine struggled to make a living, taking various jobs to support her art. Over time, she got tired of being a "starving artist," went back to school and became a successful psychotherapist. Continuing the process of her self-actualization, she eventually became a psychoanalyst. Maxine became my first close friend in Seattle and she remains a treasure in my life.

Another cherished friend, Meredith, is herself a professor in the School of Art, where she is a noted specialist in French architectural history. Even though the School of Music and the School of Art are located literally opposite each other, I may never have met Meredith through ordinary academic circumstances. It was truly a delightful coincidence that brought us together. As it happened, we both were members of the IMA, a sports facility that had an Olympic size swimming pool. One day, the lady handing out towels in the women's locker room asked if I would like to meet someone from the School of Art. "Sure," I said. This kind lady thought that maybe two young assistant professors, one from Art and one from Music, might like to be introduced. She was right. For the next thirty years, Meredith and I met at the IMA during our midday regular exercise routines. Since our lockers were adjacent, we combined getting dressed before returning to our offices, eating a quick lunch, and enjoying many special conversations.

Of course we would meet outside the IMA as well, but, as I would tease Meredith, "Our friendship is based on twenty minutes of conversation, five days a week, for thirty years."

Finally, in 1995, I met a very special friend through ordinary academic activities, but we became friends for non-academic reasons. Mona, a professor in the English Department, and I were both serving on a university committee comprising faculty from across the campus. What piqued our mutual interest in meeting outside the committee was fashion. Mona was always exquisitely dressed. Both her clothes and her jewelry were a delight to behold. Evidently, she had a similar impression of my attire. "Well," she said one day, "it would be nice to make a new friend after all that committee work!" Our friendship has now continued for many years, nourished by a multitude of interests and experiences.

In Seattle, not only have I been blessed with new friends, but my love life also has continued to blossom. I met my second husband, Robert, a few years after I arrived. In my wildest imagination, I would never have imagined that seven years later we would begin living together and then marry. Why was this a crazy notion? Well, first of all, he was fourteen years younger and had a much freer lifestyle, one which was not locked into a specific career path. He certainly had serious interests which he pursued, and was a gifted musician, a voracious reader, a self-taught engineer, and someone who was experimenting with the application of computer technology to the visual arts.

Because of his somewhat countercultural approach to life, Robert had time to pursue his interests with little concern for job security (he did have a job) or the usual bourgeois life agendas. Coming out of my somewhat European-influenced East Coast background with its emphasis on work, career, and accomplishment, Robert and his bohemian friends might well have come from another planet. Nevertheless, we became kindred spirits, transcending our differences and forging a very rich partnership and life together. It is somewhat ironic, given his lack of business training, that Robert became a successful entrepreneur. A gifted inventor and designer, he established himself as a pioneer in the field of neurotechnology (inventing light/sound machines, which can affect the brain in multiple ways) and is president of his own globally recognized company, MindPlace.

Robert and I slowly became friends, since he was well informed about computer music and clearly pleased that the UW faculty now included a composer of electronic music. A talented percussionist, he offered to play the third percussion part in my *Songs on Chinese Verses*. He began to tell me about his latest project, namely, designing a digital synthesizer. We took occasional walks and discussed our latest creative projects; we attended special lectures or films together; we met for tea at the Dawn Horse Depot, an alternative bookstore. Clearly, we had interests in common. After five years of friendship, the promise of a deeper relationship gradually dawned on both of us. What we did not know was how powerful a role this new relationship would play in each other's lives and work.

A year after Robert and I began living together, I returned to composing electronic music. This time I had my own private studio. Thanks to his natural capabilities as an audio engineer, Robert began assisting me with the technical components of my electronic compositions. During subsequent years of our work together, his imaginative collaboration became truly invaluable. I had found, unexpectedly, a true artistic partner.

After we were married and people would ask how we met, the answer was, "we met in an electronic music studio." While the School of Music at the University of Washington had no formal courses in electronic music, it did have a small Buchla analog studio in the basement where informal teaching sessions were given by a staff person. Having no experience with a Buchla studio, I decided to occasionally visit these sessions as my schedule permitted. This informal class consisted mostly of young men, including auditors. It was here that I encountered Robert for the first time. He was keenly interested in new music and often attended Contemporary Group concerts, especially when my music was being performed.

Coincidentally with my meeting Robert, a very interesting older man used to visit me in my office. He had no professional ties to the university but, rather, was so interested in new music that he became a devoted follower of the Contemporary Group programs. He was clearly delighted to discover the music of this new composer on the faculty and enjoyed stopping by my office for a brief conversation. It seems that I now had a little fan club. Although I did not know it at the time, this gentleman was Bill, Robert's father, a man who would become my father-in-law. Our shared interest in music and technology created a strong bond among the three of us. It was great fun to travel to international computer music festivals such as those in Vancouver, British Columbia and Aarhus, Denmark where my music was being performed, with my husband and father-in-law. Imagine having a new family in my life that shared my creative world!

Eventually, Robert's life took some dramatic turns. Being extremely inventive and creative, he began to design his light/sound machines at a time when the field of neurotechnology was very young. Putting his inventions on the market, his company and its products soon received critical acclaim. The young entrepreneur was now a successful business-man and a pioneer in the field of light/sound technology. I sometimes remembered the concerns expressed by my friends at my initial involve-ment with a younger, bohemian man. "You know, he is very smart and very gifted," I would say with a smile, "When he decides what he wants to do, he will accomplish it."

Of course I was happy that Robert had found his true path as an inventor and designer. Over the years, his business made increasing demands on his time and energy, including annual trips to Hong Kong and various cities in Europe. He was immensely busy and preoccu-pied. Even though we continued to nourish our marriage with occa-sional excursions and some wonderful trips to Europe, Asia, and the Southwest, there were also darker times when his demanding schedule and financial worries separated us emotionally. Although our marriage would not continue, our special years together and the intense happi-ness we experienced created a bond that continues into the present.

After my divorce in the late 90s, I remained single for about five years. At some point I decided it might be nice to find a new com-panion, and so I joined a dating service (now part of the new social culture). It wasn't long before I read the profile and watched a video of another member. Ironically, this person was also a UW professor whose field happened to be Slavic linguistics. His name was Herb. We began to meet for coffee at the Burke Museum on campus, finding it very easy to communicate about a variety of subjects and developing an easy rapport with each other. While our backgrounds were quite dissimilar — Herb was born in a small farming town in southern Colorado and had worked as a geologist prior to taking up studies in Russian — we enjoyed many of the same activities such as plays, concerts, walking, and yoga. Also, our temperaments seemed very complementary. Herb was generally relaxed and calm by nature, I was more intense.

It was very interesting for me to learn more about his work in Slavic linguistics and to hear about his academic experiences at the University of Illinois and Fordham University in New York. Also Herb's schedule was relatively simple and open since he was now retired, while I was still teaching. The culture of his farm-based Western childhood also had its influence on his personality. He was a quieter, gentler, more relaxed type of man than I had previously known. In many ways, this was "just what the doctor ordered." We began to enjoy an interesting and comfortable lifestyle together, frequently taking delightful holidays. Sometimes we were joined by my brother and his Russian sweetheart, both doctors. They would travel from Ottawa to meet us in such places as Palm Springs and Pasadena where they would attend medical conferences highlighted by tennis matches!

These were very sweet years for me because of Herb's presence and love. I had no way to anticipate what was to come. In 2006, I became mysteriously ill. It started with my feeling increasingly exhausted by and disinterested in my job. I attributed my exhaustion to academic burnout brought on by more than thirty years of teaching combined with my professional life as a composer. Before long, I decided to retire. But this did not solve the problem. I was feeling very strange, not well, and decided to sell my home and move with Herb into a retirement community. After consultation with doctors, it was determined that I was suffering from a serious depression and various drugs were prescribed. This protocol was continued for nearly two years during which time I became worse, lost twenty pounds, and was not functioning normally.

Friends and family became increasingly concerned as I was clearly going downhill and seemed a shadow of my normal self.

Finally, with the intervention of my sister Mona in Los Angeles and my physician brother Laurence in Ottawa, I was brought to the attention of a new young psychiatrist in Seattle. I still remember what she said after my first appointment: "You have the most serious kind of biologic depression. The good news is that it is highly responsive to treatment." The treatment she referred to was ECT, electro convulsive therapy. These treatments were performed on me at frequent intervals by her colleague, over a period of one and a half years. As I slowly began to recover, the frequency of treatments was reduced. Finally I no longer had to undergo ECT and continued on maintenance dosages of particular drugs.

At the time of writing this memoir, I feel well and am deeply grateful to these wonderful and caring doctors who are responsible for restoring my health. I am also most grateful to my siblings and those special friends who managed my care during a very dark period in my life when I was essentially helpless. What makes me especially happy is that Herb remains my dear companion. I feel very fortunate that we are together. As I reflect back on my life, I think that I have been lucky in love.

Several of my relationships show the central role played by a shared passion for music and the arts. It has been extremely important to me, especially at a younger time in my life, to live with men who were deeply aware of my creative goals and temperament. It was equally important for me to understand and share their creative aspirations. The same goes for many of the friends I've made in the course of my life. One of the mysteries is why such an ambitious life is chosen in the first place. An artistic profession can often be difficult, demanding, and frustrating. It's not exactly a simple case of finding a job to pay one's rent. For myself and many artists I know, it is really not a choice. To a certain extent, we are driven to pursue this life path. In essence, we love to do our creative work, we need to do it. It is a source of tremendous satisfaction, meaning, and fulfillment.

Once in a while, I have tried to understand and imagine a totally different way of living, especially since I have enjoyed occasional friendships with people who live entirely different lives than my own. They appear carefree and spontaneous, almost like birds alighting upon different trees. I am also reminded of a famous old Curtis Mayfield song, *Do be do be do*, which articulates a contrast between doing and being. Of course, in the presence of nature we are often reminded of an apparent spontaneity and ease, which human beings rarely possess. When I discovered the following poem by Emily Dickinson with its whimsical description of the natural world, I thought it would be a fitting way to close this chapter.

> The grass so little has to do –
> A sphere of simple green,
> With only butterflies to brood,
> And bees to entertain,
>
> And stir all day to pretty tunes
> The breezes fetch along,
> And hold the sunshine in its lap
> And bow to everything;
>
> And thread the dews all night, like pearls,
> And make itself so fine, —
> A duchess were too common
> For such a noticing.
>
> And even when it dies, to pass
> In odors so divine,
> As lowly spices gone to sleep,
> Or amulets of pine.
>
> And then to dwell in sovereign barns,
> And dream the days away, —
> The grass so little has to do,
> I wish I were the hay !

Chapter Six

A SPIRITUAL ODYSSEY

… A mysterious, slowly-unfolding journey
with an astonishing, even magical destination…

Program Note, *UnfoldEntwine*

At heart, I am a free spirit and my spiritual journey has included diverse explorations and experiences. The idea of a divine spark within each of us, and my sense of awe and enchantment with the world, were primary motifs in my early development. The central quest in my life for what is authentic, inspiring, and dynamic for my own inner growth has never ceased. This quest is often nourished by literature from various traditions. Two texts, one a complete poem, the other an excerpt, by the great Sufi mystic Rumi, beautifully express my longing:

All day I think about it, then at night I say it.
Where did I come from, and what am I supposed to be doing?
I have no idea.
My soul is from elsewhere, I'm sure of that,
And I intend to end up there.
This drunkenness began in some other tavern.
When I get back around to that place,
I'll be completely sober. Meanwhile,
I'm like a bird from another continent, sitting in this aviary.
The day is coming when I fly off,
But who is it now in my ear who hears my voice?

Who says words with my mouth?
Who looks out with my eyes? What is the soul?
I cannot stop asking.
If I could taste one sip of an answer,
I could break out of this prison for drunks.
I didn't come here of my own accord, and I can't leave that way.
Whoever brought me here, will have to take me home.
This poetry, I never know what I'm going to say.
I don't plan it.
When I'm outside the saying of it,
I get very quiet and rarely speak at all.

Translation by Coleman Barks

Inside my Self I discover
The scent of the Friend in every breath
Why not hold this Self close every night?

Translation by Kabir Helminski

Growing up, I was educated in the Jewish religion of my family. I was very fortunate as a child to have three living grandparents who told me dramatic stories of their lives as Russian or Polish Jews. Starting anew when they came to America in the early decades of the twentieth century was not easy for them. The courage, perseverance, and love of my grandparents made possible a new and better life for their children and grandchildren. I am deeply grateful to them. Although my parents were both observant Jews, they related to the tradition in different ways. My mother was a believer who had profound religious experiences. She was also keenly interested in other spiritual perspectives. My father, in contrast, was essentially an atheist whose primary focus as a Jew was cultural and intellectual. He had a tremendous knowledge of history, including biblical history. A natural lecturer, he volunteered to teach Sunday school when we lived in Texas. True to form, he thoroughly intimidated the little kids in his classroom, including Nina and me.

While I was being educated in the Reform Judaism practiced by my parents, I was also creatively inspired by both eastern and western texts.

I composed musical settings for psalms from the Old Testament when I was sixteen, and also set excerpts from the Bhagavad Gita when I lived in Israel. A pivotal element in my spiritual growth was my introduction to the work of Sri Aurobindo by Alexander Uriah Boscovich, my Hungarian composition teacher. In fact, Boscovich dedicated his last piece to this great twentieth century Indian yogi, philosopher, mystic, poet, and political revolutionary.

Returning to the States in 1964, I was not quite ready to embark on any serious spiritual study. Many years later, however, now settled in Seattle, I found out that a lecture about this iconic spiritual master would be given at the Theosophical Society Book Store. The person giving the lecture, Madhav Pandit, was a distinguished scholar, writer, and yogi from Pondicherry, India, a major center for the Integral Yoga and a city where both Sri Aurobindo and The Mother had resided. I was so affected by the sheer presence and magnetism of this speaker that I asked Ron, the young American who had introduced him, whether there was a Sri Aurobindo Study Group in Seattle. "Yes," he said, "I have one and we meet every week." I immediately began attending. As it turned out, the Seattle home where meetings were held became unavailable. "We can meet at my house," I announced. Thus began a long connection with participants and friends interested in the Integral Yoga of Sri Aurobindo that has lasted to the present day and has enriched my life immeasurably. Over the years, we have studied many different works by Sri Aurobindo, including *Savitri*, the longest prose poem in the English language. How fortunate that I was in the Theosophical Society Book Store on that particular afternoon when Madhav Pandit, on a national book tour, was giving his lecture!

I remain an active member of this group to the present time. Our weekly meetings include the study of various texts by Sri Aurobindo and his spiritual companion, The Mother, as well as meditation. In addition to my primary spiritual path, I have been inspired by other practices and teachers, such as Buddhism, Taoism, Eckhart Tolle, Adyashanti, and others.

An account of what I call "my spiritual odyssey" is perhaps best traced through the variety of texts that I chose for musical settings during many years of composing. Even the titles for some of my non-vocal works were taken from specific texts that sparked my imagination. These titles would come into my mind either prior to the composition of a piece, or during the actual creative process. It is only in retrospect that I understand how much these titles and the images they evoked in my imagination reveal about the direction of my inner landscape. I will now describe several works that delineate this trajectory.

As a teenager, I had written a theatre piece for solo voices, small chamber ensemble, and dancers using a text by Chaim Nahman Bialik, the grandfather of modern Hebrew poetry. In the mid-1980s, I returned to Bialik's poetry, choosing a text to be set for soprano and tape for the noted Spanish singer, Montserrat Alavedra. Prior to this piece, most of my music employed a non-tonal harmonic language. For this work, however, I decided to incorporate some Sephardic style melodies and compose with an unabashed tonal palette. The text, *Levadi* (Alone), provides a luminous description of the revolutionary impact of the Haskelah, or Jewish Enlightenment, on European Jewry. The text is also a poignant depiction of the sadness of a mother losing her child: "She trembled with anxiety over me, her son, her only son." Was I, perhaps, identifying with this historical event on a more personal level? The poem had exceptional resonance as I was increasingly drawn to spiritual paths different from those of my family tradition.

In 1999, I was asked to compose a choral and tape work using a text by Walt Whitman. His poem, *Unseen Buds*, given below, suggested to me the complex, infinite, and mystical unfolding of life. Its myriad forms and inexorable rhythm as expressed by the poet are devoid of religious connotations. At the same time, I felt a profound spiritual impulse implicit in Whitman's brief poem and this was its primary attraction for me.

Unseen Buds

Unseen buds, infinite, hidden well
Under the snow and ice, under the darkness,
in every square or cubic inch,
Germinal, exquisite, in delicate lace, microscopic, unborn
Like babes in wombs, latent, folded, compact, sleeping:
Billions of billions, and trillions of trillions of them waiting,
(On earth and in the sea—the universe
—the stars there in the heavens,)
Urging slowly, surely forward, forming endless,
And waiting ever more, forever more behind.

In 2007, I was invited by Eric Banks, conductor of the well-known choral group The Esoterics, to select a text from ancient Hindu literature and set it for a cappella chorus. The commission required that I use both the original Sanskrit and the English translation in the same piece! After some research, I selected the Mundaka Upanishad, Chapter II, verses 10–12. In composing this piece, I became aware that my sense of closeness to the text would have been impossible to imagine at an earlier time in my life.

All This

In a supreme golden sheath, the Brahman lies,
stainless, without parts. A Splendour is That,
It is the Light of Lights, it is That which the self-knowers know.

There the sun shines not, and the moon has no splendour,
and the stars are blind; there these lightnings flash not
how then shall burn this earthly fire? All that shines
is but the shadow of His shining;
all this universe is effulgent with His light.

All this is Brahman immortal, naught else;
Brahman is in front of us, Brahman behind us,
and to the south of us and to the north of us;

and below us and above us
it stretches everywhere.
All this is Brahman alone, all this magnificent universe.

The literary work that has had the most enduring influence on my spiritual journey is the epic poem, *Savitri: A Legend and a Symbol*, by Sri Aurobindo. This work encompasses multiple domains of human consciousness and reflects the author's immense knowledge of Eastern and Western philosophy, metaphysics, religion, and literature. It is a luminous, mantric, and comprehensive articulation of both human and yogic experience. In Sri Aurobindo's words:

> The tale of Satyavan and Savitri is recited in the Mahabharata as a tale of conjugal love conquering death. But this legend is, as shown by many features of the human tale, one of the many symbolic myths of the Vedic cycle. Satyavan is the soul carrying the divine truth of being within itself but descended in the grip of death and ignorance; Savitri is the Divine Word, daughter of the sun, goddess of the supreme Truth who comes down and is born to save; Aswaspati, the Lord of the Horse, her human father, is the Lord of Tapasya, the concentrated energy of human endeavor that helps us to rise from the mortal to the immortal planes; Dyumatsena, Lord of the Shining Hosts, father of Satyavan, is the Divine Mind, here fallen blind, losing its celestial kingdom of vision, and through that loss, its kingdom of glory. Still, this is not a mere allegory, the characters are not personified qualities, but incarnations or emanations of living and conscious Forces with whom we can enter into concrete touch and they take human bodies in order to help man and show him the way from his mortal state to a divine consciousness and immortal life.

I fell in love with Savitri when I first encountered the work in 1978 through the Sri Aurobindo Circle in Seattle.

It is not always easy to explain my intense interest in spiritual matters to friends who are not so inclined. On one occasion I was at an intimate dinner party with a former colleague of mine, a distinguished violinist. His son, who now lived in Dharamsala, India where he had become a friend of the Dalai Lama, was returning to Seattle for a brief visit. Knowing that I was interested in such matters, he asked, "Why do you meditate?"

"I meditate for the mind," I replied. "I wish to enter into a different relationship with my own consciousness through quieting my mind." No doubt, this was not an experience that was familiar to him, but he wanted to find a way to understand why his son had so fervently embraced an eastern practice. What happened a few months later was amazing. Thanks to the special connection his son had with the Dalai Lama, my colleague and his wife had a private visit with this eminent spiritual figure. After this, his son's commitment to a different lifestyle and tradition was no longer a mystery to him. The following excerpt from Savitri elucidates the process of meditation:

> In moments when the inner lamps are lit
> And the life's cherished guests are left outside,
> Our spirit sits alone and speaks to its gulfs
> A wider consciousness opens then its doors;

Over the years, I have used certain words or phrases from this poem as titles of pieces, such as that of my orchestral work, *The Golden Messengers*. My violin and piano piece, *Silver Deer* (1981), for example, was inspired by the following excerpt:

> Moon-bright thou livest in thy inner bliss,
> Thou comest like a silver deer through groves
> Of coral flowers and buds of glowing dreams,
> Or fleest like a wind-goddess through leaves,
> Or roamest, O ruby-eyed and snow-winged dove,
> Flitting through thickets of thy pure desires
> In the unwounded beauty of thy soul.

In addition to Savitri, Sri Aurobindo wrote many other works that continue to inspire me, including a large number of sonnets. Here is my favorite:

Krishna

At last I find a meaning of soul's birth
    Into this universe terrible and sweet
I who have felt the hungry heart of earth
    Aspiring beyond heaven to Krishna's feet

I have seen the beauty of immortal eyes,
    And heard the passion of the Lover's flute
And known a deathless ecstasy's surprise
    And sorrow in my heart forever mute.

Nearer and nearer now the music draws,
    Life shudders with a strange felicity,
All nature is a wide enamored pause
    Hoping her lord to touch, to clasp, to be.

For this one moment lived the ages past,
The world now throbs fulfilled in me at last.

I often marvel at the many threads in my life which have connected music, spiritual exploration, and personal life. Clearly, the first thread was my introduction to the Upanishads and the Vedas by my childhood composition teacher, Robert Strassburg. Meeting Alexander Uriah Boscovich in Israel and sharing a mutual interest in Sri Aurobindo's work with Joel was another important thread. Then, in 1978, while he was visiting the United States, I had the great privilege of meeting M.P. Pandit, Secretary to The Mother, Sri Aurobindo's spiritual collaborator. These various threads have woven the tapestry of my life for more than fifty years. In addition to the artistic and spiritual influences of this magical odyssey, my personal life has been immeasurably enriched by many enduring friendships which resulted from a shared quest for spirit and soul.

Chapter Seven

MY CREATIVE PROCESS

Music shall find thee in the voice of swords,
Beauty pursue thee through the core of flame

—SRI AUROBINDO

Although I have been composing since childhood, I still find the creative process elusive, fascinating, and mysterious. It is like an eternal lover I cannot live without. While this statement may sound extreme, it articulates the intense connection I have with my creative work. I believe this need is hardly unique. For many creative artists, deep commitment to their work is almost a way of existing.

For me, the composing process is essential to my process of self-discovery and to feeling alive. Each piece is a tremendous, even daunting, adventure — a pursuit of the unknown. The creative process involves, even requires, a temporary withdrawal of my mind from the ordinary world and a diving into a more intuitive consciousness. As I become immersed in the challenges posed by specific compositional material and the inevitable difficulties that emerge as a new piece is unfolding, I enter into a realm of uncharted territory. Here, I am alone.

I set up a new creative challenge in each piece. Sometimes this challenge is writing for a less familiar instrument, or for a more complex medium, or utilizing new technological tools. In other instances, sustaining coherence and interest over the duration of a longer piece constitutes my major creative objective. A third challenge is composing music in a collaborative environment and meeting the requirements of other artists.

Naturally, there are many different approaches to composing, and I have always been curious about the creative process of other artists, as well as my own process. Today, the challenge for composers in choosing an approach is magnified by the radical shifts and revolutionary changes that have taken place over the past century. The changes began when tonality, the primary language of music for centuries, was overturned by a small group of European innovators whose works had a huge influence on American composers. Viennese composer Arnold Schoenberg invented a new and revolutionary system, the 12-tone method, which was embraced, expanded, and elaborated by Schoenberg's brilliant pupils – Alban Berg and Anton Webern. The works of all three composers became foundational in establishing new modes of compositional organization, especially in the domain of pitch. Using this new approach, which prescribed certain a priori decisions about compositional structure, composers were no longer dependent on the use of a tone center or triadic harmony. Rather, the 12-tone method as well as the use of atonality represent daring new ways in which a composition's pitch structure might be organized. Stravinsky's *The Rite of Spring* (1913) and Schoenberg's *Drei Klavierstücke*, OP 11 (1903) illustrate dramatic new approaches to the organization of pitch and timbre.

Interestingly, Schoenberg's method was not "cast in stone." Some composers employed a more generalized form of the 12-tone method known as "serialism." This approach simply indicated that a series or row determining pitch, rhythm, or timbre was chosen to give the composition a degree of internal coherence. Another approach was known as "atonality" – a term that designates an even freer organization of the pitch domain. All of these newer approaches to compositional structure may be grouped under the heading "top-down," since major decisions are made before the actual compositional process begins.

Of course, not everyone suddenly stopped writing traditional (tonal) music. The idea of using tonal melody as a primary compositional element remained essential to the thinking of many composers. Eastman, for example, remained an emphatically traditional school during the middle decades of the twentieth century, and students were not generally introduced to advanced compositional techniques and contemporary repertoire. I remember my professor, Dr. Louis Mennini, hunched over in a chair and smoking a cigarette, asking his young composition students, "Where's the tune?" This is one example of a bottom-up approach to composing, i.e., starting with a specific local event and using it as a generating technique.

By contrast, the faculty composers at Princeton were dedicated proponents of Schoenberg's method, and many students at Princeton embraced a rigorously theoretical or mathematical approach to composing. Sometimes an entire composition was determined by an a priori scheme of pitch or rhythmic organization — a clear example of a top-down approach. I found it ironic, given this milieu, to hear my eminent teacher, Milton Babbitt, say that he didn't care "if composers look into the sunset to get their inspiration." I was also relieved by Mr. Babbitt's remark, since I myself was not a rigorous 12-tone composer.

Living in the bastion of twelve-tone theory and composition, I often found myself at odds with the party line. But even Anton Webern, an icon of the Second Viennese School, did not necessarily maintain the integrity of his rows. The problem with how some composers used the 12-tone method was that their work, at times, served primarily as an instantiation of a system. As far as I was concerned, in some cases there was little aesthetic substance, simply a lot of formal pretentiousness and boring music. The program notes, with their elaborate descriptions of the compositional techniques employed, could be more interesting than the pieces.

It was not only within the culture of 1960s serialism that the music itself did not live up to the elegance of its intellectual descriptions. When I took my twentieth century theory class at SUNY – Binghamton to a performance of works by John Cage, the antithesis of a 12-tone composer, the students were utterly baffled by what they were hearing and whether it counted as music. The extensive program notes, describing the amplification of soft acoustic sounds in a room with strategically placed microphones, failed to persuade them. Except for a general description of Cage's aesthetic and philosophy, I had deliberately not given my students much preparation for their concert experience and had withheld my views, believing that all approaches are to be respected.

When we returned to class after the concert, I asked them about their impressions. Neither the aural experience of very soft, slow, random sounds, nor its intellectual underpinnings made sense to them. This is often my own experience. Here I will suggest an analogy with conceptual art. The fascinating intellectual or philosophical underpinnings of a work do not necessarily translate into interesting music. The ability to think *about* sound — theoretically, metaphorically, or analytically — is not identical with the ability to think *in* sound. I feel that superior compositions utilize both these abilities. As Pierre Schaeffer, an icon of the early twentieth century *Musique Concrète* school wryly observed, "Music is meant to be heard."

In the interests of being original, some composers have sought out and executed their own versions of "modern music." There are a number of well-known composers — among them Pauline Oliveros, Morton Feldman, and Brian Ferneyhough — who bring to their work very distinctive aesthetic and philosophical premises. A listener would probably be well-advised to have some preparatory knowledge of the composer's artistic objectives and techniques at the beginning through the reading of program notes. As with all art, however, if the listener/reader chooses to reject all creative premises at the outset, it may become unlikely for him/her to actually "like" a piece. There is no doubt that the twentieth and twenty-first centuries were and are extremely interesting and challenging times to be a composer!

I have mentioned these different approaches to the compositional process because I am intrigued, and sometimes influenced, by how other composers and artists create their work. The intellectual and aesthetic foundations of their creative processes are often relevant to the types of work they make and its artistic quality. The "elephant in the room" in this discussion is the role of the unconscious during the creative act. While technique and craft are essential to any creative endeavor, these can never replace intuition and imagination. The most striking affective qualities in a piece of music are rarely explained by analysis.

Long before language acquisition, infants and babies hear implicit affective content in sounds and in speech. These sounds may be soothing, familiar, and comforting, or tense, agitated, and threatening. The aural environment of a child plays a significant role in its neural development. I was extremely sensitive to aural stimuli at an early age, and this sensitivity continues to the present. Notwithstanding extensive training and professional experience, I still listen to music and sound with primal curiosity, opprobrium, or pleasure. Naturally, I have developed other modes of listening as well, but these do not negate the earlier, more basic, modes. How we listen, how we take in sound stimuli, how we cultivate expanded ways to hear and make sense of music, especially modern music, was a subject explored in one of my theory courses.

For me, the affective, or emotional, qualities evoked by a musical work are paramount. The flashes of creative inspiration that make a piece truly arresting and memorable do not necessarily arise from the analytic part of the brain. This does not mean that musical analysis is unimportant. It means that this most abstract art cannot be fully explained in verbal or quantitative terms. It also means that the act of composition, in my experience, is not purely intellectual. What can be analytically understood is the syntactic component of a piece: its modes of progression, association, reference, and vocabulary. These are what explain its coherence, or lack of coherence. Musical compositions may be well crafted and skillful, but not necessarily interesting, let alone evocative or memorable.

A fundamental reason that composing remains central to my inner development is that it engages and integrates many levels of my consciousness. I often try to induce a kind of spaciousness and silence in my mind during the creative process. It is almost as if I am listening attentively for the composition to reveal itself. Each new work is an adventure into the unknown since my creative process is not formulaic, but organic. While I may sketch out the architecture of a composition, I never construct a work from a set of predetermined schemes. Rather, the piece becomes a living presence with whose musical components I enter into a dialogue. I utilize a variety of techniques depending on specific parameters of a work — its medium, duration, projected large scale structure, and other concerns.

My music is often inspired by visual, spatial, kinetic, or literary experience. For example, in composing pieces scored for an acoustic instrument in combination with an electronic part, I often write the synthesized music first, conceiving it as a kind of background painting into which I layer the acoustic music. As the latter is being composed, I revise elements in the existing electronic landscape, or I work on acoustic and electronic music in tandem. It is as if I am thinking of sound visually. Feeling a connection with writers, I enter into dynamic and unforeseen directions with my musical ideas, as if they were characters with a life of their own. This analogy was corroborated when I heard a well-known writer explain during a radio interview that "I never knew how my novels were going to end. What's the fun, anyway, if all an artist is doing is filling in the dots!" While I do not know exactly where my musical materials (characters) will take me, or how my pieces will end, I do know when I am convinced by a particular compositional choice.

My program notes, always written after a work is completed, try to recapture and distill the creative process unique to that composition. For example, my solo electronic work, *UnfoldEntwine*, commissioned by the International Computer Music Association in 1998, was conceived as:

> *A mysterious, slowly unfolding journey with an astonishing, even magical, destination that would appear much later in the compositional narrative. The sense of the unknown — the unforeseen – the invisible – was present in my mind throughout the compositional process, motivating a trajectory of sonic events. The single stream of sound which opens the piece ultimately devolves, after a series of briefer digressions, into multiple, concurrent tributaries. The processes of unfolding, disclosing, interleaving and entwining, which characterize the architecture of the work, also suggested its title.*

68

Deciding on the title of a composition in advance sometimes helps me to crystallize my thoughts about how to begin. Such was the case with *Masks of Eternity*, a solo electronic work conceived as a concert piece in four movements, or a series of four dance tableaux. "The striking and powerful masks displayed in the Museum of Northwest Indian Art in Juneau, Alaska, made an unforgettable impression on me in 1993. It seemed that behind the forms and frozen expressions of these remarkable artifacts lay worlds of human experience that could still resonate in the imagination of the viewer." While composing this work, I kept visualizing the masks and remembering the associations they evoked. In collaboration with choreographer Hannah Wiley, I sought to compose a piece that could be projected kinetically and dramatically as a set of mythic images, which are progressively disclosed and dynamically articulated.

Rarely has a metaphor from nature played such a central role in my compositional process as it did in *Estuaries of Enchantment for oboe and computer-realized sound.*

The image of an estuary – an arm of the sea that extends inland to meet the mouth of a river, or the part of the wide lower course of a river where the current is met and influenced by the tides – greatly informed my delineation of both timbral content and temporal flow in the electronic part of this work. At moments dramatic, portentous, complex; at other moments transparent, gentle, even meditative – this evanescent otherworld with its churning flow of currents, densities, rhythms, and its shifting sonic content, simultaneously enfolds and embraces a solitary instrumental trajectory. While the oboe music is presented at times in discrete melodic gestures as foreground of a large, swirling, sonic canvas, at other times it is heard enmeshed or encircled by the intense electronic flow. Structured in two distinct sections – the first opens with a rapid, dramatic burst, the second with a minor triad quietly enveloped in sounds of nature – the music gradually moves towards a dissolution of all its multiple tensions and interior streams.

> *At the end, both oboe and electronic music seem to merge in unexpected, radiant peace.*

Sometimes I begin a composition without a title in mind. Unexpectedly, I may have an experience which helps me to crystallize my thoughts into particular symbolic images. Such was the case with *Through Amber for clarinet and computer-realized sound.*

> *I began with a draft of the electronic music imagined as a kind of ancient, aural prism — dense, material, warm in color — yet permeable by intense light. The term amber came to mind because of these associations and also because it symbolized the embodiment of an ancient living essence frozen in time. Then, while on a professional trip, I had the opportunity to visit the Toronto Art Museum. The highlight of my visit was the arresting and spectacular sculpture in the Henry Moore Gallery. As I walked through the incredible assemblage of these huge mythic figures placed in the center and around the room, I became aware of my own movement. Its directions, returns, pauses were impelled by a desire to re-enter the alluring symbolic worlds evoked by the power, beauty, and mystery of specific sculptures. The image of a solo dancer moving in a vast, fluid, primordial landscape thus became a compositional metaphor for the relation of live performer and electronic sound. Indeed, some of the initial material in the clarinet part is derived from the electronic music and elaborated in various ways. The slow passage of time is intended to capture the listener's attention and focus it on the delicate sonic choreography, which connects two distinct timbral worlds.*

In *The Palaces of Memory for Chamber Orchestra and Tape,* my compositional inspiration was enriched by the following story told by Matteo Ricci, a sixteenth century Jesuit priest. This individual brought to China a wonderful memory system that had been used in the West since the days of ancient Greece. To improve their powers of retention, people would build memory palaces, huge imaginary buildings they kept inside their heads. "*To everything we wish to remember,*" wrote Ricci, "*we should give an image; and to every one of these images we should assign a position where it can repose peacefully until we are ready to reclaim it by an act of memory.*"

What intrigued me about this story was the recognition that one of the powers music possesses for me is the capacity to evoke and capture images of feeling, being, and knowing, and to crystallize these images into sonorous forms. As we move through the world of a musical work, our experience is transformed into memory.

The previous paragraphs have described aspects of my creative process within individual compositions. They answer some of the questions listeners to my music have posed, such as: "Where do you get your inspiration?" "What is it like to compose? "How do you begin a piece?" "How do you imagine sounds?" Reflecting on this deeply familiar activity, I am struck by its complex motivations. Part of the fascination and challenge in writing each new piece is to confront my insecurity and anxiety. This element of the process is often distressing and uncomfortable.

I remember a statement in a book on the creative process that made me laugh with recognition. The writer was describing the acute distress many artists feel when they are trying to begin a new work or experiencing a creative block. Referring to himself, he said that when the discomfort of not working exceeded the terror of working, he was compelled to begin. It's like entering a fiery furnace or starting a treacherous mountain ascent. The artist is driven to such pursuits. The creative process can bring elation and ecstasy, as well as anxiety and even despair. These feelings are documented in the letters of composers throughout history.

I began this chapter by stating that I find the creative process elusive, fascinating, and mysterious. I shall close the chapter with a beautiful Chinese story called *The Secret of the Wood*. I think that this story eloquently communicates the mystery and ineffability of the creative process.

Once, Chuang Tzu tells us, there was a master craftsman who made such beautiful things out of wood that the king himself demanded to know the mystery of his art.

"Your highness," said the carpenter, "there is no secret, but there is something. This is how I begin: When I am about to make a table, I first collect my energies and bring my mind to absolute quietness. I become oblivious of any reward to be gained or any fame to be acquired. When I am free from the influences of all such outer considerations, I can listen to the inner voice, which tells me clearly what to do.

When my skill is thus concentrated, I take up my axe. I make sure that it is perfectly sharp, that it fits my hand and swings with my arm. Then I enter the forest.

I look for the right tree, the tree that is wanting to become my table. And when I find it I ask: 'What have I for you, and what have you for me?' Then I cut down the tree and set to work.

I remember how my masters taught me to bring my skill and my thought into relation with the natural qualities of the wood."

The King said, "When the table is finished, it has a magical effect on me; I cannot treat it as I would any other table. What is the nature of this magic?"

"Your Majesty," said the carpenter, "what you call magic comes from what I have already told you."

ff

Chapter Eight

CONFRONTATION AND COLLABORATION:
TECHNOLOGY AND THE COMPOSER'S ART

"I hope you're not going to write any of that terrible electronic music."

—HOWARD HANSON, COMPOSER

It is with a sense of irony that I describe my personal journey into the world of electronic music. As an undergraduate at the Eastman School in the early 1960's, a very conservative school at the time, I had no access to electronic studio classes or professors who were engaged with this new medium. I do remember going over to the renowned Sibley Library on my own to engage in the somewhat subversive act of listening to the early electronic works of Karlheinz Stockhausen. As described in Chapter Two, I was totally surprised when Howard Hanson, president of the Eastman School of Music, approached me on the day of my graduation at the University of Rochester and made the remark quoted above. How ironic that these words, spoken to me in June 1963, would turn out to be amazingly prescient.

In the intervening years, 1963–68, I would study composition in Israel with the renowned composer and teacher Alexander Boscovich, and then with George Rochberg, head of the music department at the University of Pennsylvania. My work was entirely acoustic during these years since electronic resources were unavailable. My later work at Princeton, however, would profoundly affect my life, both internally and externally.

At the time I began my studies in 1968, Princeton was one of two universities in the entire country (the other one being Stanford) that offered computer music courses. Several composers on the faculty were writing computer music and their works were receiving acclaim. To appreciate what it meant to begin working in this new field, one must understand that an enormous amount of time and attention was spent learning various computer programs which would allow composers to structure wave forms on a fundamental level. Rather than composing with given sounds – e.g. the sound of a clarinet, flute, cello – students had to be willing to learn how to create timbre on a granular level. This took a great deal of time and patient experimentation. Did I "like" the timbres I had created? Not necessarily. I would often have to go back to the drawing board.

To further complicate and exacerbate the difficulties of the whole process, it should be pointed out that, after having typed all my information on punch cards using Princeton's 360-91 mainframe computer, I had nothing to show for my efforts but a digital tape with thousands of numbers representing the wave forms. To convert the digital tape to sound, it was necessary to make another three-hour round trip to Murray Hill, New Jersey, where Bell Labs had a digital to analog converter. Whew! To say the least, the whole process was extremely tedious, tiring, and frustrating.

One might ask, why did I continue to pursue this research? After all, there was no requirement that graduate students at Princeton learn computer music. What was happening for me, however, was that my entire compositional process was being stimulated and challenged. On a very deep level, I was beginning to think about the domain of timbre and the compositional process itself in entirely new ways. For example, not only was I experimenting with new approaches to the structuring of wave forms which were, in effect, the sounds of my piece, I was also looking to more fully integrate the pitch and timbral dimensions of the composition. When a specific a priori pitch organization had been determined, I would structure my wave forms to reflect this tonal organization, thus integrating the piece on a deeper compositional level.

Conversely, the minute changes that determined the timbre of sounds could also serve as a template for structuring pitch.

This kind of original thinking about music and sound were the direct result of my challenging studies at Princeton. While the demands of early computer synthesis were sometimes stressful and discouraging, the process of learning through experimentation was also exhilarating and exciting. I could easily identify with scientists working on difficult projects in a lab and then arriving at an "aha" moment. Eventually this work would impact both my written PhD dissertation, *Toward Structural Characterization of the Timbral Domain*, and its compositional exemplification, *Polyvalence for Computer and Ensemble.*

My first job after completing my doctoral degree at Princeton was at SUNY-Binghamton in upstate New York. Since no facilities were available for writing computer music, I found myself using an analog studio for the first time. In some respects, this experience was liberating, since working with the Moog synthesizer was a real-time process. It was like being in an environment where a certain number of already-determined sounds were provided. It was up to the individual composer to transform these sounds and to create interesting compositional structures.

When I joined the faculty at the University of Washington in 1977, the department was, as mentioned earlier, definitely not sympathetic to electronic music. The only opportunity to access electronic technology was in the small analog studio located in the basement and taught by a staff instructor. While I was curious about the Buchla equipment, which was used by a number of students, I decided that the best option for me was the creation of my own private studio. My home in Lake Forest Park had an open area in the backyard surrounded by beautiful trees. Here I built an electronic studio, which housed a number of technological tools, including software and hardware as well as recording equipment. In this private studio, I would write a number of pieces over several decades. These works included those for synthesized sound alone and those that combined electronic sound with live performance. In addition, I continued to write acoustic music, often using the spacious music room inside my home with a grand piano and recording equipment. I was very fortunate to have all these resources so conveniently accessible.

In the appendices, I include a critical discussion of a number of my electroacoustic works by Elizabeth Hinkle-Turner in her excellent book, *Women Composers and Music Technology in the United States* (2006). In addition, excerpts from the liner notes of my two monographic recordings by critic George Gelles are given.

Throughout my tenure at the university, I had the good fortune of encountering, either through their music or in person, a number of internationally-recognized European composers. These included English composer Jonathan Harvey, French composer Jean-Claude Risset, and Finnish composer Kaija Saaraiho. Their compositions, with which I became well-acquainted, included *Mortuos Plangos/Vivos Voco* by Harvey, *Little Boy Suite* by Risset, and *Io* by Sarraijo. In Europe, these ultra-modern composers were often supported by their governments in national centers for electronic music. Their experimentation was extremely important to me and a stimulating reminder that my inner musical world was connected to a much larger compositional universe.

Of course, it is always incumbent upon composers to use new resources with musical imagination. In 1992, I was invited to join a panel on electronic music at the annual meeting of the College Music Society held in San Diego. Various pioneers in the field were chosen to speak, in particular, ninety-year-old Otto Luening. The highlight of this unique symposium was a program commemorating the first concert of electronic music held at New York's Museum of Modern Art in 1950. What astonished me was that the best pieces on the program were created with more rudimentary, early technologies, while some less interesting works were composed using quite sophisticated tools.

Clearly, the creative imagination of the composer will always play a central role in the quality of a composition. There can be a danger in what I term "the sorcerer's apprentice syndrome," where the seductiveness of sophisticated tools overrides the composer's creative talent and aesthetic discrimination. Sometimes, the program notes and the composer's description of all the fancy technological bells and whistles used in a particular piece are far more interesting than the piece itself. As English composer Trevor Wishart has noted, "Aesthetic developments are made possible, but not defined, by technological developments."

Another truism was colorfully expressed by my friend and colleague, noted Hungarian conductor Peter Eros. Quoting his mentor, Erich Leinsdorf, and smiling impishly, Peter said, "Lack of talent lasts forever."

Because a comprehensive body of theory does not yet exist that explores, defines, and evaluates this new repertoire created with a dazzling array of technological tools and innovative compositional premises, it is especially incumbent upon the listener to approach these modern works with an open perspective. Just as it took some time for the paintings of Joan Miro, Jackson Pollack, and other original artists to be accepted and understood, the true masterpieces of electroacoustic music may also need further dissemination and critical analysis to be fully appreciated.

Given the remarkable growth in technology since the early twentieth century and the equally remarkable variety of ways in which composers apply these technological tools, I am struck by the illuminating words of Marcel Proust with which I close this chapter: "The true voyage of discovery consists not in seeking new landscapes but in having new eyes."

NOTE:

The title and content of this chapter are based on the Solomon Katz Lecture in the Humanities I gave in 1996 at the University of Washington. In preparation for that lecture I had the opportunity to review not only my own history in electronic music, but also to reflect upon many developments of the technological tools available to composers and how individual composers employed these tools.

Chapter Nine

CODA: REMINISCENCES OF A MAGICAL LIFE

"Immeasurable being wells up in my soul"

—SRI AUROBINDO

Part of what makes my life feel extraordinarily magical are the encounters that were completely unforeseen and momentous, as in the case of my professional life, or enchanting, in terms of my personal life. Meeting an incredible mentor when I was twelve is an example of the former type of encounter. Meeting Joel at the Eastman School when I was seventeen, marrying when I was twenty-one, living in Israel with Joel and studying with Boscovich, is an example of an exceptionally happy, enriching, and adventurous chapter in my life.

While there are always surprises, I have wished to focus on those encounters that elevated, enhanced, and expanded my world in significant ways. Of course, the great loves of my life are part of that story. It is also true that a number of rare professional opportunities unexpectedly came my way. For example, a fortuitous accident of timing resulted in my becoming the first woman to receive a PhD in Music from Princeton and the first woman to write computer music. These distinctions would never have come to me had it not been for a casual conversation with an acquaintance I met on a train. When I saw her sixteen years later at a composers' conference, I walked over to thank her, explaining, "That conversation with you changed my life."

I still find it remarkable that, as a young, relatively traditional composer, I was transformed – by an apparently serendipitous circumstance and my resulting exposure to computer synthesis at Princeton – into a forward-looking, technology-oriented, mature composer. Moreover, my personal trajectory intersected in advantageous and amazing ways with the major revolution taking place in electronics, providing composers with a wealth of new technological tools. In my wildest dreams, I could never have imagined the exciting career that would unfold – a career that would take me to Europe, Israel, India, Canada, and cities throughout the United States. Had I been born a decade earlier, this would never have happened. I was part of a generation of composers privileged to discover a marvelous new world.

Looking back, I see how amazing coincidences, serendipitous connections, and unforeseen events opened for me a world rich with adventure, privilege, friendship, and love. I also recognize that there is a central theme uniting the diverse chapters of my life. This is my passion for music. Thus, it seems fitting to end this memoir with a poem by Franz von Schober, which Schubert beautifully set to music. It is one of my favorite Schubert songs.

AN DIE MUSIK

Du holde Kunst, in
wieviel grauen
Stunden,
Wo mich des
Lebens wilder
Kreis umstrickt,

Hast du mein Herz
zu warmer Lieb'
entzünden,
Hast mich in eine
bessere Welt
entrückt!
in eine
bessere Welt
entrückt!

Oft hat ein Seufzer,
deiner arf'
entflossen,
Ein süsser, heiliger
Akkord von dir

Den Himmel bess'rer
Zeiten mir
erschlossen,
Du holde Kunst,
ich danke dir dafür!

Du holde Kunst,
ich danke dir!

TO MUSIC

O lovely art, in
how many grey
hours,
When life's
mad tumult
engulfs me,

Have you kindled
my heart
with ardent love,
Have you
transported me
to a better world!
Transported into
a better world!

Often has a sigh
flowed out from
your harp,
A sweet, divine
harmony from you

It unlocked for me
the heaven of
better times,
O lovely Art,
I thank you for this!

O lovely Art,
I thank you!

Appendix 1

Women Composers and Music Technology in the United States (2006)

—ELIZABETH HINKLE-TURNER

A highly respected composer and teacher, Diane Thome (b.1942) began studying piano when she was seven and a half and composing when she was eight. It wasn't until she was a graduate student at Princeton University in the late 1960's that she became interested in contemporary electronic media. Although she is an accomplished pianist, Thome does not normally perform and has only occasionally been the pianist for her own pieces which include solo, chamber, orchestral, and electroacoustic works.

Thome received a PhD and an M.F.A. in composition at Princeton University working with Milton Babbitt and becoming the first woman to receive a doctorate in 1973. Additionally, she holds an M.A. in theory and composition from the University of Pennsylvania and two undergraduate degrees with distinction in piano and composition from the Eastman School of Music. After three years as an assistant professor at the State University of New York in Binghamton, she accepted a position at the University of Washington in 1977 where she is currently a professor and chair of the composition program. From her earliest days at Princeton, Thome worked almost exclusively with computer synthesis. Her doctoral dissertation, *Toward Structural Characterization of the Timbral Domain,* illustrates her concern with specific tone color and structure, elements which can be closely controlled by a composer using the computer. In a 1995 article, however, Thome credits work done on the Moog analog synthesizer at SUNY-Binghamton as having an important impact on her music since it allows her freedom to improvise in a 'hands-on' manner with electronic controls and to physically shape different sounds. The dominant element of her electroacoustic composition became the sound itself.

In the same article, she describes some of her earliest experiences with computer music, focusing on a 1973 work, *Night Passage*, done in collaboration with two women – film and kinetic sculpture artist, Judith Vassallo, professor at the Moore College of Art in Philadelphia, and German choreographer and dancer Birgitta Trommler. Designed for "*Seven Dancers in Zones of Fire, Earth, and Water,*" the piece evolved through various discussions about its formal structure within which each artist had a great deal of freedom to work independently. Once completed, *Night Passage* featured the dancers moving in sculptured areas of earth, fire, and water, while audience members could walk freely through this performance space. Thome's music for the event was computer-synthesized using the Music V and Music 360 programming languages.

When interviewed by Beverly Grigsby in 1983, Thome divided her electroacoustic music into three distinct categories: works which use synthesized sound alone; works which combine synthesized sound and traditional instruments; works which add recorded and electronically manipulated instrumental sounds to live instrumental music and synthesized materials. The infinite variety of relationships possible in the third category especially intrigues the composer, and in all her electroacoustic music, taped and live sounds are closely interwoven. An excellent example of this is her *Anaïs (1976) for cello, piano, and tape*, which is an homage to the diarist Anaïs Nin. All three elements in the piece overlap in their phrase beginnings and endings, and share many abstract melodic and harmonic ideas. At times their parts are quite distinct timbrally, making the work an interesting study of opposites.

Thome has also created effective settings of voice and tape. Her *Levadi (Alone) for soprano and tape* (1986) is based on a poem by Chaim Nachman Bialik, a Russian-Jewish writer of the Jewish Enlightenment. Thome had actually written a ballet inspired by another poem of this writer when she was fourteen years old. Treating the tape accompaniment in a similar manner to the way one might write for voice and piano, *Levadi* features melodies recalling the Sephardic Jewish tradition. The tape part also provides contrasting melodic and rhythmic ideas which flow in an improvisatory manner when heard alone. A later work, *The Ruins of the Heart (1990) for soprano, orchestra, and tape*, utilizes translations of poems by the Sufi poet Rumi. In this piece, the listener is presented with two different media in combination with the text. The tape part is heard alone in three extended, highly ornamented, and dense passages of contrasting material. These sections serve as a reflective and atmospheric commentary on the text.

Thome's works for solo tape are fewer in number, but also explore the timbral possibilities of electronically transformed acoustic and synthesized sound. Her 1994 *Masks of Eternity* begins with synthesized marimba-like sounds. A dramatic and other-worldly quality is evoked by the 'almost real' sonic materials. *Masks* is in four parts and was inspired by the Native American masks displayed in the Museum of Northwest Indian Art in Juneau, Alaska, which made a strong impression on the composer. Metallic sounds are also featured, and an ambient environment of wind textures is used, giving a sense of being swept into the past while striving towards the future. This sense of timelessness is also evident when hearing her *UnfoldEntwine for solo tape*. A fifteen minute work commissioned by the University of Michigan for the 1998 International Computer Music Conference, *UnfoldEntwine* uses multiple streams of sound that constantly change in timbral content and intensity. The continual development of these sounds makes for a compelling and introspective piece.

Thome's *Like a Seated Swan (1999) for viola and computer-realized sound* involves the use of changing viola timbres and ideas against a continuous electronic part. The computer-realized portion of the work is similar in character to *UnfoldEntwine* in that the rich digitally recorded and altered, sustained viola tones are subjected to minute timbral permutations to produce a continuously-changing atmosphere. The violist performs a virtuosic and abstract part which alternately plays in contrast and in combination with the tape. Like her other instrumental works described earlier, the tape part is so closely integrated with the live instrumental music that the boundaries between instrument and tape are often blurred and obscured. *Like a Seated Swan* was commissioned by the Seattle Symphony and written for Seattle Symphony violist Dorothy Shapiro who has performed it on numerous occasions, including the International Viola Congress held at the University of Washington in 2002.

All of Thome's electroacoustic music from her earliest work to her current projects is intricate and intriguing in its construction. Each piece illustrates the composer's ability to create an enormous palette of sound featuring timbres with minutely changing differences. Abstract in nature, her music is quite beautiful and shows the variety of her poetic, visual, and philosophical interests and influences, as well as her aesthetic concern with creating pieces in which the technology does not dominate the compositional process but enhances it instead. Centaur Records has recently released a second monographic CD of her recent electroacoustic works, *Bright Air/Brilliant Fire*, which takes its title from a 1997 piece for flute and computer-realized sound. Her most recent work, *Estuaries of Enchantment for oboe and electronics*, commissioned by the Eleusis Consortium, was premiered during the University of Washington's computer music concert in May, 2002.

Appendix 2

A clue to the music of Diane Thome can be found in her taste for the visual arts. Strikingly, a note about these pieces arrives on a card that displays Joan Miro's "Beautiful Bird Revealing the Unknown to a Pair of Lovers," one of the miraculous Constellations from the early 1940s. Miro shows a self-contained universe, resonant with mythic symbol, profuse in image and incident, subtle in its sure sense of balance and order, yet despite these aspects of rigorous intellect, almost hedonistic in its ample and evident delight in creation.

Much the same can be said about Diane Thome's music. Listening to this collection which provides an aural snapshot of her work over a span of 18 years, you are struck, first of all, by their consistency of voice. Over the course of a generation that has turned the teachings of the academy on its head — stylistic conformity has been replaced by a Babel of voices — Ms. Thome has stayed true to her ideals. Now as then, her works spring from a rich soil of poetic imagery found in words and in artifacts alike; now as then, they display a compositional sophistication that is generous in acknowledging other music yet unswerving in its own integrity; now as then, they concern themselves less with meeting an audience on its own level than in raising it to hers....

—FROM *Palaces of Memory*, CENTAUR LABEL CD 2229, 1995

Having composed music with synthesized sound for more than a quarter century — her first pieces in the medium date from the 1970s — Diane Thome has created a corpus of uncommon distinction. The reference works tell you that Ms. Thome is the first woman to write computer-synthesized music, but this information is of secondary import. Of primary significance is that Ms. Thome writes a music that is intensely poetical, impeccably crafted, and elevated in artistic purpose. It weds compositional probity with a lyrical imagination that is stimulated by – and that in turn further evokes – a richness of literary and visual metaphor. To respond to this music's attractiveness and allure is rewarding, but it is doubly rewarding to accept its implicit invitation to let the imagination range more widely still…

—FROM *BrightAir/Brilliant Fire*, CENTAUR LABEL CD 2527, 2001

Former Executive Director of the Philharmonia Baroque Orchestra, George Gelles was music and dance critic for the Washington Star from 1970 to 1976 and Contributing Editor of the Britannica Book of Music. He has contributed numerous articles to the New Grove Dictionary and has written extensively on music and dance subjects for The New York Times, Musical America, Ovation, and other publications.

Appendix 3

ENTERTAINMENT & THE ARTS, *SEATTLE TIMES*
SUNDAY, NOVEMBER 24, 2002

"For Diane Thome, this retrospective will be an electrifying milestone"

—BY MELINDA BARGREEN, SEATTLE TIMES MUSIC CRITIC

Diane Thome is accustomed to being the only woman in the room.

Over the years since she emerged from Princeton as that rarity of rarities, a woman composer who specializes in computer music, Thome – now on the faculty at the University of Washington – has made her way as one of few women in a male-dominated field.

It doesn't bother her a bit.

Thome (whose name starts with a soft "th" like "thin" and rhymes with "home") turned 60 this year, and that occasion will be marked with a major retrospective of her work at a Contemporary Group Concert Dec. 2 in Meany Theatre (7:30 pm, 206 – 543-4880). The retrospective spans 23 years of Thome's work.

The 60-year milestone doesn't bother Thome, either, because she doesn't look or act 60. Always stylish-looking, she projects an air of self-possessed serenity, but Thome is far from aloof; she has a lively sense of humor and a great laugh. Her studio in the basement of the UW Music Building, with its view of grass and trees, is filled with neatly arranged files that have background info, program notes, lyrics and other details of her compositions. Looking over the flier for her concert, Thome mulls over some of the roads taken that have brought her to this milestone.

"This is a wonderful time for me as a composer," she says.

"Singers lose some ability as they grow older, but composers can mature."

"I've had to battle here and there to be taken seriously as a woman composer. But it never fazed me. There were times I wasn't totally confident, but I've been so committed to composition, and I've been so lucky to have many wonderful, supportive people behind me."

Thome was only eight when she decided to be a composer, and she never wavered from that decision. By 12, she was "writing little pieces for some kind of contest," which she won, telling her mother she now had to have a composition teacher.

"Luckily for me, my mother found a wonderful teacher, Robert Strassburg. To have a great mentor is a huge gift. He would take pieces of mine and enter them in contests without my knowledge, and I'd get scholarships to study in the summer with composers like Roy Harris and Darius Milhaud."

Not all great composers are good teachers, but Thome says hers were very encouraging. Her studies at Aspen and Tanglewood encouraged her to apply to the Eastman School of Music in Rochester, N.Y.

"Eastman was a very traditional school, so I wrote more traditional music," Thome remembers. "But at Tanglewood (in the summer) I had become fascinated with the atonal works of Schoenberg. I played a Stravinsky/Schoenberg piano recital from memory and received the highest possible rating, even though I wasn't a serious pianist – I think it was because the piano professors were all terrified of that music."

The real turning point in Thome's career was her arrival at Princeton, where she earned her PhD. Applying at the suggestion of a friend – Thome never expected to get in – but on April Fool's Day 1968, the mailbox brought her not only a letter of acceptance, but a fellowship and more money than she had ever imagined.

It was at Princeton that Thome met up with composer Milton Babbitt, a big influence in her academic life. She wasn't interested in composing 12-tone music, which was Babbitt's forte. "It was a very rigorous place," Thome remembers of Princeton in the late 1960s.

"It was really a boys club. But that didn't bother me, because I was used to being in places where there were no women."

At Princeton she first got hooked on electronic music, at a point where computers were so large they occupied whole rooms and had to be shared by different users. Worse, the computer programs were tedious to learn and soon became obsolete.

Thome, fascinated by the emerging technology, persevered to become the first woman PhD in Composition at Princeton (following an M.F.A. at that school, and an earlier M.A. in theory and composition from the University of Pennsylvania). At one point, then married to composer/conductor Joel Thome and living in Philadelphia, she had to drive a six-hour round trip to Murray Hill, New Jersey where Bell Labs had a D to A converter.

"I'm thrilled with what's happening now: so much acceleration and efficiency," Thome says of today's computer music technology.

She was ready to go out in the world five years after arriving at Princeton, and Thome says, "That degree spoke for me as well as my music." For a while she taught at the State University of New York in Binghamton, but changes in the scope of her position made her want to move. That's when she came to the University of Washington in 1977, leaving behind "everyone and everything I knew. I was ready for my life to be different. I needed more quiet; I wanted to be near the water, and part of a large faculty of composers and performers."

A large body of chamber, choral, orchestral, and solo music – much of it inspired by poetry – attests to Thome's considerable range as a composer. Not all of it is electronic music; some, including an upcoming premiere for the local choral group, The Esoterics, is purely acoustic. Most often, though, her scores combine live acoustic performance with computer-synthesized music; she usually writes the electronic portion first, and then the acoustic part.

Every piece was born through different technology. "Masks of Eternity," a 1994 piece for solo tape, used a Kurzweil 2000 digital synthesizer and Cakewalk for Windows sequencing software; the sections were digitally mixed using the MTU Microsound digital/audio system. The 1998 "UnfoldEntwine" was created primarily with a Capybara-66 signal processing system in conjunction with Kyma 4.5 software, with additional software all running on a Power Mac. The new "Estuaries of Enchantment," for oboe and computer-realized sound, melds the tones of the oboe with synthesized music run on a Macintosh Cube.

Thome's music has been described as "high modernist…searching, intense, and full of integrity." Her music is so diverse – atonal and tonal, electronic and acoustic – that it's hard to characterize in a single phrase. What she usually does is to expand the sonic possibilities of live performance by creating computer-generated sound that underscores and sets off what the onstage performers are doing.

The rich viola sound of "Like a Seated Swan" for viola and computer is overlain with sounds that are delicate, eerie, and string like, floating as the swan does. Thome describes "UnfoldEntwine," a solo electronic work, as a "mysterious, slowly-unfolding journey" in which a single stream of sound diverges into multiple connecting sounds, all interweaving with each other.

"UnfoldEntwine," "Estuaries of Enchantment," "Masks of Eternity" and three others ("Pianismus," "Bright Air/Brilliant Fire," and "The

Yew Tree") will all be heard in the Dec. 2 concert at Meany. Thome will be "an excited member of the audience," but she won't be on the stage behind any keyboards.

"The piano is a tremendous education," she explains, "but I never wanted to be a concert pianist. I'm actually pretty shy."

Appendix 4

SELECTED WORKS

Alexander Boscovich Remembered (1978) – violin, piano, tape

All This (2004) – a cappella chorus

Anaïs (1976) – cello, piano, tape

And Yet… (2006) – viola and computer-realized sound

Angels – (1992) virtual reality artwork for computer

Bright Air/Brilliant Fire (1997) – flute/alto flute, tape

Cassia Blossoms (1988) – soprano, flute, clarinet, violin, viola, cello, piano, harp

Celestial Canopy (2000) – orchestra

Estuaries of Enchantment (2002) – oboe and computer-realized sound

Indra's Net (1989) – orchestra

Into Her Embrace: Musings on Savitri (1991) – solo tape

January Variations (1973) – solo tape

Levadi (1985) – soprano and tape

Like a Seated Swan (1999) – viola and computer-realized sound

Los Nombres (1976) – piano, percussion, tape

Lucent Flowers (1988) – soprano and chamber orchestra

Masks of Eternity (1994) – solo electronic work

Night Passage (1973) – environmental theatre piece

Pianismus (1982) – solo piano

Polyvalence (1972) – six players and computer

Ringing, Stillness, Pearl Light (1988) – piano and tape

Silver Deer (1982) – violin and piano

Songs on Chinese Verses (1979) – soprano, flute, clarinet, violin, viola, three percussion

Spiral Journey (1986) – solo piano

Stepping Inward (1987) – oboe/English horn, viola, mandolin, guitar, harp

Sunflower Space (1978) – flute, piano, tape

The Golden Messengers (1985) – large orchestra

The Palaces of Memory (1993) – chamber orchestra and tape

The Ruins of the Heart (1990) – soprano, orchestra, tape

The Yew Tree (1980) – soprano, large chamber ensemble

Three Psalms (1979) – baritone, mixed chorus, flute, harp, violin, viola, cello

Three Sonnets by Sri Aurobindo (1984) – soprano, orchestra

Through Amber (2001) – clarinet in A and computer-realized sound

To Search the Spacious World (1978) – viola, piano, tape

UnfoldEntwine (1998) – computer-realized solo electronic work

Unseen Buds (1996) – mixed choir and computer-realized sound

Veils – solo tape

Winter Infinities – chamber ensemble, tape

Appendix 5

RECORDINGS

All This – a cappella choir – The Esoterics – Terpsichore Records CD

Bright Air/Brilliant Fire – electroacoustic music by Diane Thome Centaur CD CRC 2527

Los Nombres – for piano, percussion, tape – Tulstar Records, LP

Palaces of Memory – electroacoustic music by Diane Thome Centaur CD CRC 2229

Pianismus for solo piano – Sunbursts – solo piano works by 7 American women – Leonarda Productions; LE345, 1998 – LP

Polyvalence for Six Players and Computer – New Directions in Music – Significant Contemporary Works for the Computer – Tulsa Records, LP

Prestidigitation – And Yet ... for viola and computer-realized sound, Melia Watras – Fleur de Son Classics CD

The Ruins of the Heart – soprano, orchestra, tape – Composers in the Computer Age – Centaur CD RC 2144

Three Psalms for baritone soloist, mixed chorus, flute, harp, violin, viola, cello – Capstone Records, Society of Composers, Inc. CD – "America Sings" Boston Musica Viva

Lightning Source UK Ltd.
Milton Keynes UK
UKOW02f1330280916

284011UK00001B/219/P